NOV 2

MAR

Mar

JAN

MAR 18

FL-28-2

JAPANESE-AMERICAN INTERNMENT IN AMERICAN HISTORY

David K. Fremon

Enslow Publishers, Inc.

44 Fadem Road	PO Box 38
Box 699	Aldershot
Springfield, NJ 07081	Hants GU12 6BP
USA	UK

Dedicated to Sir William and his friends

Library of Congress Cataloging-in-Publication Data

Fremon, David K.
    Japanese-American internment in American history / David K. Fremon.
       p. cm. — (In American history)
    Includes bibliographical references and index.
    Summary: Includes personal accounts to describe the period in American
history when Japanese Americans were detained in internment camps; also,
discusses the issues and controversy surrounding the decision.
    ISBN 0-89490-767-0
    1. Japanese Americans—Evacuation and relocation, 1942-1945—Juvenile
literature. [1. Japanese Americans—Evacuation and relocation, 1942-1945.
2. World War, 1939-1945—Personal narratives, American.] I. Title.
II. Series.
D769.8.A6F74 1996
940.53'1503956073—dc20   96-753
                                      CIP
                                      AC

Printed in the United States of America

10 9 8 7 6 5 4 3

Illustration Credits: National Archives and Records Administration,
pp. 6, 9, 42, 107; War Relocation Authority, pp. 13, 15, 16, 20, 25, 27,
36, 44, 47, 51, 52, 60, 63, 77, 84, 98, 103, 108, 111; Courtesy Library
of Congress, *The Dictionary of American Portraits*, published by Dover
Publications, Inc., in 1967, p. 32; Japanese American Citizens League,
p. 40; White House photo, p. 115.

Cover Illustration: War Relocation Authority; National Archives

★ CONTENTS ★

JAPS

On December 7, 1941, Shigeo "Shig" Wakamatsu planned to sleep late. The twenty-seven-year-old *Nisei* man (American-born person whose parents were from Japan) kept a busy schedule. While studying at the College of Puget Sound, he worked as a night watchman and receiving clerk at Tacoma's farmers' market. He could use the rest.

Instead, he got a jolt. A fellow Nisei stormed into the market and yelled, "'Hey, Shig, the Japs are bombing Pearl Harbor!' By the time I turned around, he was gone, he was so excited," Wakamatsu recalled years later.[1]

A startled Wakamatsu dressed hurriedly, then went to a local restaurant. "One of the owners was screaming, 'By God, when we're through, we're gonna kill every Jap!'" Wakamatsu said. "Then he saw me. 'No, Shiggy, we're gonna save you,' he promised."[2]

For Shigeo Wakamatsu and thousands of others in America, the Pearl Harbor bombing altered their lives completely. They were first generation Japanese-born Americans (*Issei*) or second generation American-born Nisei. Although their ancestry was Japanese, they were as American as the Italian-American fisherman, the Irish-American dockworker, or the southern-born farmer. Yet solely because of their ancestry, their patriotism was questioned. For many Americans, the bombing by the Japanese of the United States Naval base at Pearl Harbor in Honolulu, Hawaii, turned innocent Japanese Americans into monstrous, subhuman "Japs."

Wakamatsu and other Japanese Americans worked

On December 7, 1941, the Japanese bombed Pearl Harbor, a United States Naval base in Hawaii. Smoke billows out of the battleship U.S.S. Arizona, *stationed in Pearl Harbor.*

to destroy that image. The following day, they called for a special assembly at their college. Students listened to the radio as President Franklin Delano Roosevelt declared the Pearl Harbor invasion on December 7, 1941, "a date which will live in infamy." A friend handed Wakamatsu a piece of paper as they listened. The paper contained the Japanese-American Creed, written only months earlier.

SOURCE DOCUMENT

Yesterday, December 7, 1941—a date which will live in infamy—the United States of America was suddenly and deliberately attacked by naval and air forces of the Empire of Japan. . . .

Japan has, therefore, undertaken a surprise offensive extending throughout the Pacific area. The facts of yesterday speak for themselves. The people of the United States have already formed their opinions and well understand the implications to the very life and safety of our nation.

As commander in chief of the Army and Navy I have directed that all measures be taken for our defense. . . .

I ask that the Congress declare that since the unprovoked and dastardly attack by Japan on Sunday, December 7, a state of war has existed between the United States and the Japanese Empire.

On December 8, 1941, President Franklin Delano Roosevelt spoke to Congress to ask for a declaration of war against Japan.

After the president's speech, Wakamatsu addressed the student body, ending his speech with the creed. The last paragraph of this document read:

> Because I believe in America, and I trust she believes in me, and because I have received innumerable benefits from her, I pledge myself to do honor to her at all times and in all places; to support her Constitution; to obey her laws; to respect her flag; to defend her against all enemies, foreign or domestic; to actively assume my duties and obligations cheerfully and without any reservations whatsoever, in the hope that I may become a better American in a greater America.[3]

His patriotism should have gone unquestioned. Instead, Shig Wakamatsu and others ended up as domestic prisoners of war. In May 1942—one month before his scheduled college graduation—he was relocated to a detention camp in the Rocky Mountains.

Wakamatsu was not alone. More than one hundred twelve thousand Japanese Americans—seventy thousand of them Nisei—were evacuated from the West Coast in 1942. These children, women, and men were placed in ten relocation centers, mostly in desolate Rocky Mountain sites. Many lost their careers; most lost their property. Although none was ever found guilty or even accused of a war crime, all were treated as if they were traitors.

Even more disgraceful than the government's action was the reaction of their fellow Americans. During the time of the evacuation, no California

Chieko Hirata
Period II, English I

My Last Day At Home

The month of May when I was attending school, all the residents of Hood River county, as well as the people of the whole western coast was surprised to receive such an unexpected order of evacuation.

Promptly after hearing about the order I with my folks went to register and then for a brief physical examination. Then I helped my folks pack and prepared to leave my dear home on May 13, 1942.

On May 8, 1942 I withdrew from Parkdale Grade School, where all my friends and teachers bid me farewell with sorrowful face and tears. Our packing never seem to cease, we kept on packing then finally we were finished. Then came May 13th, my most dreaded day which I shall never forget the rest of my life. On the afternoon of the 13th, I board the train headed for Pinedale, California.

On the night of the 15th we arrived. The weather was pretty hot. In Pinedale I lived in the D-section which had forty barracks, which had vie apartments to a barrack.

I stayed at the Pinedale Assembly Center about two months. Then around July 15, 1942 we received our order to evacuate for Tule Lake. Then on July 18th we evacuated for Tule Lake and spent a night on the train. I arrived in Tule Lake. At present I am living in Block 58. The residents of this block is most Tacoma folks which I am not very much acquainted with as yet. Being that my cousin lives in Block 57 I am always visiting them.

I am always hoping that this war will end, so that I will be able to go back to Parkdale, my home town and see all my old friends, and live to my dying days in my old home in Parkdale, Oregon.

Herbert Yoshikawa

A student writes about his early experiences at a relocation center.

politician and few government leaders from anywhere else criticized the West Coast removal.

Earl Warren served as Chief Justice of the United States Supreme Court. As the nation's chief jurist, he later became known as a defender of individual rights. But as California attorney general in the early 1940s, he spearheaded the drive to oust Japanese Americans from their homes. A regretful Warren was later quoted as saying, "[the evacuation of Japanese Americans was] one of the worst things I ever did."[4]

ALIENS INELIGIBLE FOR CITIZENSHIP

When Commodore Matthew Perry, a United States Navy commander, met with Japan's emperor, Komei, in 1854, the emperor agreed to end two centuries of isolation and open up trade with the West. Perhaps the four American gunboats with cannon aimed at the royal palace influenced the emperor's decision.

The new treaty meant little to the average Japanese. For the next thirty years, most of the Japanese visiting the United States were sailors. They stayed in American ports only long enough to unload and load goods.

America already had Asian immigrants. Chinese workers toiled on the construction of the transcontinental railroad. Even while using Chinese workers, white Americans discriminated against them. Racist bullies harassed and even murdered Chinese immigrants.

In 1882, President Chester A. Arthur signed a bill that halted further Chinese immigration. California law forbade Chinese (as well as African Americans and Native Americans) to testify against whites in court.

This, in effect, allowed whites to steal from the Chinese. A "Chinaman's chance" came to mean no chance at all.

In the 1880s, Japanese workers came to Hawaii to harvest the sugar and pineapple crops. West Coast farms, mines, lumber camps, and railroads also sought Japanese laborers.

Most of the early Japanese immigrants were young men. Like many other immigrants, they planned only to make money and return home, but also like other immigrants, many stayed.

Farmland in the Pacific Coast states of California, Oregon, and Washington was plentiful then. Earlier arrivals claimed the best ground. The Issei took what was left. They worked wonders with this land. Japanese farms yielded crops which were as good as or better than those of white farmers.

The Japanese success startled white settlers. When those workers started owning land and competing with white Americans, many whites started panicking.

Nearly twenty-five thousand Issei and Nisei lived in the United States in 1900, almost all of them on the Pacific Coast. Another hundred thousand would arrive in the next eight years. Westerners noted the increased Japanese numbers. *The San Francisco Chronicle* decried the "complete orientalization of the Pacific Coast."[1]

Anti-Japanese campaigns stepped up after 1905, when Japan defeated Russia in the Russo-Japanese War. Membership in an anti-immigrant group, the

Issei and Nisei farmers worked wonders with the soil. Here, farmers are shown harvesting cabbage.

Native Sons of the Golden West, increased. The young Earl Warren was one of those new members. The Oriental Exclusion League sought removal of all Asian immigrants. When Japanese immigrants opened successful laundry businesses, whites started the Anti Jap Laundry League.

The San Francisco Chronicle led a barrage of racist attacks against the Japanese. Headlines warned of "THE YELLOW PERIL."[2] Soon, the city followed the newspaper. In 1906, San Francisco removed its Japanese students from white schools and ordered them to attend segregated schools in Chinatown.

The Japanese government protested. President Theodore Roosevelt made a so-called gentlemen's agreement with the Japanese government. It stated that the United States would not pass anti-Japanese laws. Japan, in turn, would stop issuing passports allowing Japanese citizens to enter the United States, except for "former residents, parents, wives, or children of residents."[3]

When the Issei became successful, they sent for their families. If they were single, they started families. Many states outlawed marriages between people of Japanese descent and white Americans, but *baishaku-nin* (go-betweens) arranged marriages between Japanese-American men in the United States and eligible women still in Japan. Often, the would-be groom knew nothing more about his bride than the picture she sent. These women became known as "picture brides."

Facing Discrimination

Roosevelt's promise did not extend beyond his term in office, and it did not include laws made by individual states. In 1913, California enacted the Alien Land Law. Aliens ineligible for citizenship were prohibited from owning land. They could rent land for no longer than three years.

This law mainly affected the Issei. The Federal Naturalization Act of 1790 allowed "any alien, being a free white person" to immigrate and become a United States citizen. After the Civil War, "aliens of

Many Japanese men in the United States married "picture brides," women they knew only by pictures they sent. The women married by proxy in Japan, then joined their new husbands in the United States.

African nativity" were also included. But Asians, including the Japanese, could live most of their lives in the United States without hope of attaining citizenship.

Their American-born Nisei children, however, were United States citizens. Many Issei avoided the Alien Land Law by putting their property in their citizen children's names. A 1920 revision to the law barred immigrant parents from serving as guardians

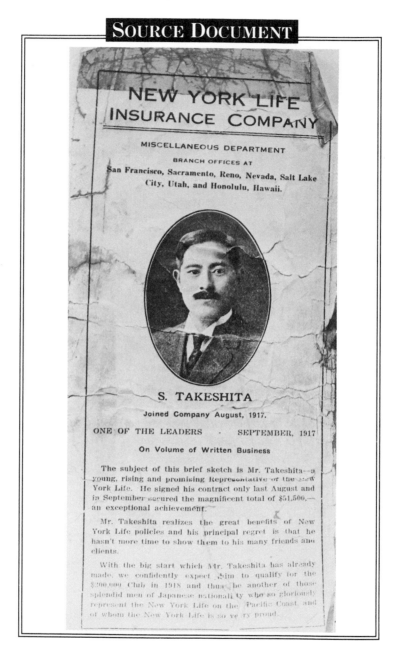

NEW YORK LIFE INSURANCE COMPANY

MISCELLANEOUS DEPARTMENT

BRANCH OFFICES AT

San Francisco, Sacramento, Reno, Nevada, Salt Lake City, Utah, and Honolulu, Hawaii.

S. TAKESHITA

Joined Company August, 1917.

ONE OF THE LEADERS · SEPTEMBER, 1917

On Volume of Written Business

The subject of this brief sketch is Mr. Takeshita—a young, rising and promising Representative of the New York Life. He signed his contract only last August and in September secured the magnificent total of $51,500,—an exceptional achievement.

Mr. Takeshita realizes the great benefits of New York Life policies and his principal regret is that he hasn't more time to show them to his many friends and clients.

With the big start which Mr. Takeshita has already made, we confidently expect him to qualify for the $300,000 Club in 1918 and thus be another of those splendid men of Japanese nationality who so gloriously represent the New York Life on the Pacific Coast, and of whom the New York Life is so very proud.

Many Japanese Americans were kept out of high-paying jobs. But if given the chance, they often excelled in their work.

for their minor citizen children and from renting their children's land.

These Japanese Americans faced countless other varieties of discrimination. Some were economic. Unofficial but very real restrictions kept them out of many professions. Japanese-American teachers, for instance, had a hard time finding work because many white parents did not want Japanese-American teachers instructing their children. Most trade unions blocked Japanese Americans from membership. Property owners in many neighborhoods would not rent or sell homes to the Japanese Americans. Shops, restaurants, and hotels would not serve them.

In Bakersfield, California, where Earl Warren grew

Unfriendly neighbors of Issei and Nisei put up signs discriminating against Japanese Americans.[4]

up, telephone directories used the word "Oriental" instead of an Asian's name before a listed telephone number. Writer Yoshiko Uchida, growing up in Oakland, California, always asked new barbers, "Do you cut Japanese hair?" She recalled an incident in which a photographer tried to crowd her, the only Japanese American in her class, out of a Girl Reserves picture. Only when a white friend insisted did the photographer include her in the picture.[5]

Sometimes treatment became violent. An Issei who opened a store had reason to fear picketing or rock throwing. In 1921, a band of white men in Turlock, California, rounded up fifty-eight Japanese Americans, put them on a train, and shipped them out of town.

Despite anti-Japanese sentiment, many Issei prospered. In California, only about sixteen hundred Issei owned farms in 1940, but those farms produced between 30 and 35 percent of all the fruits and vegetables grown in the state. They had a virtual monopoly on snap beans, celery, and strawberries. The average value per acre of farmland in California, Oregon, and Washington was $37.94. The average value of Nisei farmland, much of which was worked by Issei parents, was $279.96.

Not every Japanese-born resident was a farmer. Issei worked as domestic servants, merchants, gardeners, florists, and commercial fishermen. Many were drawn to urban life. Several West Coast cities had neighborhoods called "Little Tokyo."

The Japanese Americans helped themselves by setting up ethnic unions such as the Japanese Association. These groups provided translation and information, legal services and loans, and community events. Japanese-language newspapers, with local items and news from the homeland, provided a unifying force. Religious institutions, both Christian churches and Buddhist temples, also brought the Japanese Americans together.

Anti-Japanese agitators charged that Japanese Americans drove whites out of California. If anything, the opposite was true. Japanese-American farmers took land rejected or ignored by whites. They supplemented rather than competed with other West Coast farmers. If Japanese-American farmers had chased whites away, the population of the West Coast would have dropped. However, the population of the West Coast states more than quadrupled, from 2.4 million to 9.7 million, between 1900 and 1940. Even so, laws further diminished Japanese-American rights. The Cable Act of 1922 ruled that Asian women married to American citizens were not eligible for United States citizenship. Women who married "aliens ineligible for United States citizenship" would lose their own citizenship. Two years later, a new immigration act excluded "aliens ineligible for citizenship." This, of course, meant the Issei.

Restrictive immigration laws, added to the fact that many Japanese-American families were small, kept the population of Issei and Nisei low. In 1940,

Japanese accounted for less than one tenth of one percent of the United States population. In California, where most lived, they made up less than 2 percent of the population. By numbers, they were no threat to their neighbors.

"Little Tokyo" was a prominent neighborhood in many West Coast cities.

But Japan, their ancestral homeland, was a threat to world peace. In the 1930s, the Japanese empire invaded the Chinese province of Manchuria. Further conquests appeared inevitable. Would the Japanese ever stop their conquests? Would the Issei and Nisei living in the United States come to the aid of Japan?

As early as 1937, a Nisei college student at the University of California pondered his fate if war broke out between Japan and the United States. "Our properties would be confiscated and most likely [we would be] herded into prison camps," he predicted.[6] His words were prophetic.

WE LOOKED LIKE THE ENEMY

On December 8, 1941, the day after the Pearl Harbor bombing, *The Los Angeles Times's* headlines screamed "350 Reported killed in Hawaii Raid," and "Hostilities declared by Japanese." Congress formally declared war on Japan that day. But the unofficial war on the Issei and Nisei had already begun.

The Federal Bureau of Investigation (FBI) kept a list of potentially suspicious Japanese and Japanese-American men and women. Business owners, teachers, farmers, fishermen, journalists—anyone who might hold a leadership role—was held for questioning. Since the Japanese government donated money to Buddhist temples in the United States, Buddhist priests came under suspicion. By nightfall of December 7, hundreds of men and women were in custody.

Charles Kishiyama saw government officials take his father. "[T]hey had a struggle where they rassled with my dad, which frightened me," he recalled. "I didn't know what was going on, but they took him."[1]

These roundups of suspected saboteurs (enemy agents) were not the first actions against the Japanese population. A month before Pearl Harbor, the FBI raided the establishments of Japanese-American businesspeople and community leaders in Los Angeles's Little Tokyo. They seized records and membership lists of groups such as the Japanese Chamber of Commerce and the Central Japanese Association.

Most captured Japanese Americans cooperated with the authorities. A spokesperson for the Central Japanese Association commented, "We teach the fundamentals of Americanism and the high ideals of American democracy. We want to live here in peace and harmony. Our people are 100 percent loyal to America."[2]

Terminal Island, a small island in Los Angeles harbor, had been home to a colony of Japanese fishermen for decades. In February 1942, these fishermen and their families lost their homes, boats, and other property in only a few days. Every male who had been to Japan in recent years was placed in custody; then their families were told they had only forty-eight hours to dispose of their property and leave the island. No English-language newspaper spoke out against the forced evacuation.

Other government officials added insult to injury. State sales tax collectors went out to Terminal Island while the hapless Japanese and Japanese Americans sold everything they could at bargain rates. One former Terminal Island resident remembered, "Here we were working as if it was a matter of life and death, and [a tax collector], without any respect for our precious minutes, came over and collected to the last penny."[3]

Two days after the evacuation order, a once-prosperous community became a ghost town. An evacuee lamented, "The only souls around were the soldiers and the prowlers who were going through the empty homes."[4]

Suspected Saboteurs

"My mother was dumbfounded. She said, 'War? By whom?' First, she said 'Russia?', then 'China?' We said, 'No, Japan!'" a Nisei woman related years later. "My mother couldn't believe it. My mother was so ashamed."[5]

The woman's reaction was not unusual among the West Coast Japanese community. Many Issei, even those who strongly loved their native culture, now rejected their homeland. "Everything Japanese was bad," a woman said. "The fear struck Mother; she began tearing up Japanese books and breaking phonograph records with a hammer."[6]

Up and down the Pacific Coast, the atmosphere became chaotic. Los Angeles mayor Fletcher Bowron said "After Pearl Harbor, everything was in a state of confusion. We kept getting reports of Japanese spying and sabotage. . . . There were reports they were in touch with the Japanese fleet . . . and we didn't have any way to tell who were loyal and who weren't."[7]

Rumors, most of them absurd, spread like a California brushfire. Japanese-American fishermen were really officers in the emperor's navy. Japanese-American farmers in Hawaii allegedly planted their crops in the shape of huge arrows to direct the Japanese air force to the Pearl Harbor naval base. American university class rings were said to have been found on the fingers of downed Japanese pilots after Pearl Harbor—a sure sign that secret agents in the United States were working for the hated Japanese empire.

Residents of Japanese ancestry immediately fell victim to government rules. Their bank accounts were

Japanese-American fishermen were wrongfully accused of spying against the United States in the early days of World War II.

frozen and their safe deposit boxes were confiscated; now they had no access to their own money. They were held to an 8:00 P.M. curfew. They could not travel more than five miles beyond their homes. The government banned travel of "Japanese individuals, by plane, train, bus, or boat." They had to turn in their shortwave radios, cameras, binoculars, and firearms. Knives, including Boy Scout pocket knives and hunting knives, were forbidden.

Nisei as well as their Issei parents faced discrimination. Many Japanese Americans lost private business or civil service jobs. Patriotic Nisei who wished to enlist in the armed forces after Pearl Harbor found that their services were not desired. Many of those already in the army or navy were discharged. Later, Japanese Americans would be given the classification IV-C—enemy aliens. They got this label although they were neither enemies nor aliens. "It was not because we had done anything wrong, but simply because we *looked* like the enemy," wrote Yoshiko Uchida.[8]

What was the United States going to do about this group of suspected saboteurs? That problem led to heated debates in Washington, D.C.

We Must Worry About the Japanese

An unprepared United States military had been caught off guard by the Japanese air force on December 7, 1941. Shortly before 8:00 A.M., when Japanese bombers attacked the Pearl Harbor Naval base near Honolulu, Hawaii, more than twenty-five hundred Americans died, and another thirteen hundred were injured.

The Pacific Fleet lay in ruins. Japan's surprise raid took less than two hours, but it left the navy shattered. The battleship *U.S.S. Arizona* was totally destroyed; battleships *U.S.S. Nevada* and *U.S.S. West Virginia* lay in the bottom of the harbor. Eighteen United States ships were hit. More than two hundred aircraft were damaged.

Military and political officials refused to admit that

Japanese and other Asians in the United States often faced bigotry from nativist groups.

Japanese troops destroyed United States ships because the Americans were not alert. They did not realize that the Japanese had the capability or daring to pull off such a raid. There had to be some reason for the Pearl Harbor disaster, they figured. Spies and enemy agents must have helped the Japanese. Those spies, they reasoned, must be Japanese or Japanese Americans.

Frank Knox, secretary of the Navy, took a trip to Hawaii. He reported that Japanese Americans in Hawaii performed "the most effective fifth column [spy network] that's come out of this war, except in Norway."[9] He made the impractical suggestion that all Hawaiians of Japanese blood be removed from the Hawaiian island of Oahu.

Commander Kenneth Ringle of the Office of Naval Intelligence disagreed. His ten-page report said that the Issei and Nisei on the West Coast were no more dangerous than anyone else. Ringle got his information firsthand. He hired the Los Angeles Police Department and a safecracker to break into Japanese groups' offices and examine their records.[10]

Voices of reason were drowned out by those of wild speculation, however. A West Coast businessperson named Curtis Munson, a special investigator appointed by the State Department, reported that the overwhelming number of Japanese Americans were loyal. But he claimed that there were Japanese Americans in the United States who might tie dynamite to their clothing and make human bombs of themselves. According to Munson, "Dams could be blown and half of [Southern] California could actually die of thirst."[11]

One person who read Munson's report was John L. DeWitt, an army officer who was nearing the end of an undistinguished career. DeWitt was described as "a cautious, bigoted, indecisive, sixty-one year old army bureaucrat."[12] Staff members described him after Pearl Harbor as "gone crazy."[13]

DeWitt's statements indicated an irrational fear and hatred of all Japanese. He claimed "The Japanese are an enemy race."[14] "We must worry about the Japanese all the time until [they are] wiped off the map," he commented.[15] "A Jap's a Jap. They're a dangerous element, whether loyal or not."[16] DeWitt admitted that there were no known cases of sabotage by Nisei. He claimed that the fact that no sabotage had taken place was proof that such treachery would occur soon. FBI (Federal Bureau of Investigation) director J. Edgar Hoover attacked DeWitt's "hysteria and lack of judgment."[17]

DeWitt certainly was not the only American with rabid anti-Japanese views. But as head of the newly created Western Defense Command, he was in a position to implement them.

The Fight Over Evacuation

Assistant Secretary of War John McCloy recommended establishing restricted areas. Remove everyone suspicious, he suggested, then return those who were not deemed dangerous. McCloy wanted to let the military act "in spite of the constitution."[18]

DeWitt liked McCloy's suggestion. He urged the War Department to round up all suspects fourteen years old and up from enemy nations and to deposit them at inland locations. He urged Roosevelt to give the secretary of war the right to detain aliens when the secretary found it necessary.

DeWitt and McCloy found a foe in the Justice Department. Attorney General Francis Biddle saw no reason to remove people who were not proven to be disloyal residents. Biddle reported, "We have not uncovered . . . any dangerous persons that we could not otherwise know about."[19] Biddle's findings brought about a power struggle between the Justice Department, which opposed moving innocent civilians, and the War Department, which wanted to detain Japanese Americans.

Top War Department officials met with Biddle on February 1, 1942. The attorney general drafted a press release that read, "The Department of War and the Department of Justice are in agreement that the present military situation does not . . . require the removal of American citizens of the Japanese race."[20]

The War Department, in truth, was in no such agreement. Biddle said he would have nothing to do with mass evacuations. McCloy retorted that if it came to a choice between the safety of the country and the Constitution, "Why the Constitution is just a scrap of paper to me."[21]

Three days later, DeWitt created twelve restricted zones that covered the Pacific Coast. Enemy aliens in these zones had nighttime curfews. During the daytime, they could leave home only to go to work. If they disobeyed the regulations, they could be arrested immediately.

Secretary of War Henry L. Stimson had been wavering on the evacuation issue. By February 11, he decided to go along with the evacuations. Stimson made his recommendation to Roosevelt, who was not wholly enthusiastic about the idea. The president told Stimson, "go ahead and do anything you think necessary. But, be as reasonable as you can."[22]

The pressure from Roosevelt and Stimson was too much for Biddle. The Justice Department gave up opposition to evacuations.

Executive Order 9066

On February 19, 1942, a Nisei speaker proclaimed, "our greatest friend is a man who is the greatest living man today—President Franklin Delano Roosevelt."[23] That evening, the Nisei's "greatest living friend" was busy betraying them.

Roosevelt signed Executive Order 9066 on February 19. It was one of the greatest violations of civil rights in American history. The order gave the military authority to exclude "any or all persons from designated areas, including the California coast." Secretary of War Stimson immediately gave DeWitt authority "to carry out the duties and responsibilities

Franklin Delano Roosevelt signed Executive Order 9066 into law on February 19, 1942.

imposed by said Executive Order." DeWitt had free rein to do whatever he wanted.

The word "Japanese" never appeared in Roosevelt's executive order, yet from the beginning, Japanese were the order's only intended targets. Noncitizen Germans and Italians were "enemy aliens," too, but nobody seriously considered locking them up.

Many escaped the order because of an Italian-American fisherman in San Francisco named Giuseppe DiMaggio. Nobody outside San Francisco knew Giuseppe DiMaggio, but everyone knew his son. Joe DiMaggio was Most Valuable Player with the world champion New York Yankees. In 1941, he hit in a record fifty-six consecutive games. Force Joe Di-Maggio's father from his home? Why, that would be . . . un-American!

The Japanese in America had no national hero like Joe DiMaggio. More important, they lacked experienced national leadership. Most of the leaders among German Americans and Italian Americans were United States citizens. The Japanese leaders were noncitizen Issei, and those most influential Issei were already detained by authorities. Few of their Nisei children were over thirty years old. They lacked the experience needed to deal with governments and politicians. The most influential Nisei organization, the Japanese American Citizens League (JACL), was less than five years old.

Less than a week after the evacuation order, a Japanese submarine fired shells at some storage tanks off the Santa Barbara coast. The next night, the army detected what appeared to be an enemy aircraft flying over Los Angeles. Within a couple of hours, more than fourteen hundred shells were fired, raining down fragments that damaged dozens of cars. The "enemy aircraft" turned out to be a wayward weather balloon.

DeWitt nonetheless used the hysteria to take further action. He issued his first proclamation on March 2, 1942. It called for two military zones: Zone 1 covered the western third of California, Oregon, and Washington, and the southern quarter of Arizona; Zone 2 covered the remainder of the four states.

Authorities urged those of Japanese ancestry to leave Zone 1. There were few voluntary evacuees. They had neither the time nor the desire to sell their properties, and nowhere to go if they did. Inland, Americans seemed no more hospitable to them than were their Pacific Coast neighbors. Some were turned back by armed mobs; others were thrown in jail. Many encountered **No Japs Wanted** signs.

One major loophole kept the government from moving the Issei and Nisei. They were civilians, and the military had no control over them. Stimson went to Congress to solve this problem. He requested a law ordering any civilian who disobeyed a military order in a military zone to serve a year in jail. The bill passed unanimously.

War Relocation Authority

Most Japanese Americans were not going to leave the Pacific Coast of their own free will; that appeared obvious. But where were they going to be moved had not been determined.

Inland, governors let it be known that the exiles would not be welcome in their states. Wyoming's governor said, "If you bring Japanese into my state, I promise you they will be hanging from every tree."[24] Japanese Americans would be welcome in Idaho, that state's governor said, only if they were in "concentration camps under military guard."[25]

The Idaho governor's idea prevailed. The Issei and Nisei would be moved to inland camps. They would be kept there for an indefinite period of time, perhaps for the duration of the war.

Only the army had the force to move more than a hundred thousand civilians, but War Secretary Stimson balked at removing thirty-five thousand troops from combat to guard generally peaceful civilians. On March 18, Executive Order 9012 established the War Relocation Authority (WRA). Army troops would transport the evacuees to their relocation camps. From there, the civilian WRA would take charge. Milton Eisenhower, an Agriculture Department official and older brother of General Dwight Eisenhower, was chosen as the first WRA director. He concluded that he had no alternative but to build evacuation camps where the residents could send their children to schools, perform useful work, and maintain as much self-respect as possible. When the war is over, Eisenhower wrote, "we as Americans are going to regret the unavoidable injustices that may have been done."[26] Eisenhower soon resigned the thankless job, and his assistant, Dillon Myer, replaced him.

The War Relocation Authority had a notable ally. The Japanese American Citizens League (JACL) was working to have Nisei exempted from the evacuation, so ultimately, the JACL voted to cooperate with the WRA. Many Japanese Americans despised the decision.

Mike Masaoka of the JACL defended the decision. "If in the judgment of military and federal authorities evacuation of Japanese residents from the West Coast is a primary step toward assuring the safety of this nation, we will have no hesitation in complying," he

In the nineteenth century, groups of Issei came to the United States. During World War II, second-generation Japanese Americans were treated as enemies.

claimed. "But if, on the other hand, such evacuation . . . cloaks the desires of political or other pressure groups who want us to leave merely for motives of self-interest, we feel that we have every right to protest."[27]

Masaoka gave several reasons for his group's cooperation with evacuation orders. Cooperation could be seen as the Japanese Americans' contribution to the war effort. It would show Japanese-American patriotism and thus help non-Japanese work on their behalf. Japanese Americans had the duty to follow their alien Japanese family members if they were forced into camps.

The JACL felt they had had no real alternative. The money of most Japanese Americans had been confiscated by the government. Since most Issei and Nisei were not voting-age citizens, they had no political power. The leaders they had trusted for decades were sitting in prison camps. Public opinion was against people from the nation that bombed Pearl Harbor and appeared to be winning the Pacific war. Cooperation with the government, even in an unjust removal, was a better alternative than violence and pointless bloodshed. Historian Roger Daniels commented, "Active resistance was really out of the question. It would have been absolute community suicide."[28]

On March 27, DeWitt issued Public Proclamation Number 4. This order forced persons of Japanese ancestry to stay in Military Zone 1 after the end of the month. A few days earlier, the government had encouraged these civilians to leave the military zone.

Now, the same government was ordering them to stay.

A few days earlier, DeWitt had issued Exclusion Order Number 1. Persons of Japanese ancestry were moved from Bainbridge Island, near Seattle, Washington, to a camp in Manzanar, California. Fifty-four families, including 276 people, most of them United States citizens, were evicted from their homes. There would be more than a hundred such evacuation orders before the end of the war.

On June 2, 1942, DeWitt declared the entire West Coast an exclusion area. Half a world away, another significant event was taking place. It was June 3 in the western Pacific Ocean. The Battle of Midway, the bloodiest sea battle in the history of warfare, had begun. By the end of the battle, the Japanese fleet would be crippled. United States Naval Intelligence told Roosevelt that the Midway defeat ended any chance of a Japanese invasion of America.

If military necessity was the only reason for evacuation, it could have stopped right there. But sometimes people and governments continue mistakes rather than admit them. Plans for the mass evacuation continued as scheduled.

Many people hoped that an evacuation would not take place. "At first we did not believe the reports of a possible evacuation," recalled Shig Wakamatsu. "Then we thought, 'Maybe they will take our parents, but not us.'"[29]

Without warning, the signs popped up throughout Japanese-American communities on the West Coast. The worst nightmare of a peaceful, innocent people was coming to pass.

The signs ordered all persons of Japanese ancestry, "aliens and non-aliens" alike, to

4

WHY DID THE GUNS POINT INWARD?

report to assembly points on specific days. Those signs themselves were an insult. The term non-alien might have been used because the government was ashamed to admit that it was rounding up and detaining United States citizens. "During the war years I was never referred to as a citizen. I was always considered a non-alien," wrote Seattle-born Gordon Hirabayashi.[1]

Newspaper headlines blared "Japs Given Evacuation Orders Here." Actually, they were given little instruction. They had to meet at a central point, such as a bus station, within ten days. They were told only to bring bedding and linens, extra clothes, toilet articles, tableware, and "essential personal effects."

Hideo Murata, a World War I veteran, could not believe the notice. He called his friend the sheriff, who

WESTERN DEFENSE COMMAND AND FOURTH ARMY
WARTIME CIVIL CONTROL ADMINISTRATION
Presidio of San Francisco, California
May 3, 1942

INSTRUCTIONS
TO ALL PERSONS OF
JAPANESE
ANCESTRY
Living in the Following Area:

All of that portion of the County of Alameda, State of California, within the boundary beginning at the point where the southerly limits of the City of Oakland meet San Francisco Bay; thence easterly and following the southerly limits of said city to U. S. Highway No. 50; thence southerly and easterly on said Highway No. 50 to its intersection with California State Highway No. 21; thence southerly on said Highway No. 21 to its intersection, at or near Warm Springs, with California State Highway No. 17; thence southerly on said Highway No. 17 to the Alameda-Santa Clara County line; thence westerly and following said county line to San Francisco Bay; thence northerly, and following the shoreline of San Francisco Bay to the point of beginning.

Pursuant to the provisions of Civilian Exclusion Order No. 34, this Headquarters, dated May 3, 1942, all persons of Japanese ancestry, both alien and non-alien, will be evacuated from the above area by 12 o'clock noon, P. W. T., Saturday, May 9, 1942.

No Japanese person living in the above area will be permitted to change residence after 12 o'clock noon, P. W. T., Sunday, May 3, 1942, without obtaining special permission from the representative of the Commanding General, Northern California Sector, at the Civil Control Station located at:

920 - "C" Street,
Hayward, California.

Such permits will only be granted for the purpose of uniting members of a family, or in cases of grave emergency.

The Civil Control Station is equipped to assist the Japanese population affected by this evacuation in the following ways:

1. Give advice and instructions on the evacuation.
2. Provide services with respect to the management, leasing, sale, storage or other disposition of most kinds of property, such as real estate, business and professional equipment, household goods, boats, automobiles and livestock.
3. Provide temporary residence elsewhere for all Japanese in family groups.
4. Transport persons and a limited amount of clothing and equipment to their new residence.

The Following Instructions Must Be Observed:

1. A responsible member of each family, preferably the head of the family, or the person in whose name most of the property is held, and each individual living alone, will report to the Civil Control Station to receive further instructions. This must be done between 8:00 A. M. and 5:00 P. M. on Monday, May 4, 1942, or between 8:00 A. M. and 5:00 P. M. on Tuesday, May 5, 1942.
2. Evacuees must carry with them on departure for the Assembly Center, the following property:
(a) Bedding and linens (no mattress) for each member of the family;
(b) Toilet articles for each member of the family;
(c) Extra clothing for each member of the family;
(d) Sufficient knives, forks, spoons, plates, bowls and cups for each member of the family;
(e) Essential personal effects for each member of the family.

All items carried will be securely packaged, tied and plainly marked with the name of the owner and numbered in accordance with instructions obtained at the Civil Control Station. The size and number of packages is limited to that which can be carried by the individual or family group.

3. No pets of any kind will be permitted.
4. No personal items and no household goods will be shipped to the Assembly Center.
5. The United States Government through its agencies will provide for the storage, at the sole risk of the owner, of the more substantial household items, such as iceboxes, washing machines, pianos and other heavy furniture. Cooking utensils and other small items will be accepted for storage if crated, packed and plainly marked with the name and address of the owner. Only one name and address will be used by a given family.
6. Each family, and individual living alone, will be furnished transportation to the Assembly Center or will be authorized to travel by private automobile in a supervised group. All instructions pertaining to the movement will be obtained at the Civil Control Station.

Go to the Civil Control Station between the hours of 8:00 A. M. and 5:00 P. M., Monday, May 4, 1942, or between the hours of 8:00 A. M. and 5:00 P. M., Tuesday, May 5, 1942, to receive further instructions.

J. L. DeWITT
Lieutenant General, U. S. Army
Commanding

SEE CIVILIAN EXCLUSION ORDER NO. 34.

The evacuation order of May 1942. This poster explained the procedures that Japanese Americans had to follow and what they should bring with them when evacuated.

assured him it was real. Murata checked into a local hotel, paid for his room in advance, and killed himself. Authorities saw, clutched in his hand, a Certificate of Honorary Citizenship presented the previous Fourth of July. The certificate was a "testimony of heartfelt gratitude, of honor and respect for your loyal and splendid service to the country."[2]

Each family or person living alone had to register. Yoshiko Uchida's family number was 13453. People were given tags with their family numbers and told to show up later with all the baggage their family could carry. Then they rushed home to pack up or sell their goods.[3]

Usually, they had no choice but to sell their property for ridiculously low prices. A woman sold a twenty-six-room hotel for $500. A man, who had just spent $125 for a new battery and tires for his pickup truck, was forced to sell the entire truck for $25.

Farmers suffered more than anyone else. They had planted crops at the request of government agencies, and they hoped to be allowed to harvest them before the evacuation. The government, however, double-crossed the farmers. It forced them to vacate the land before the harvest. Thus the farmers gained none of the crops' profits but incurred all of the debts.

Because the evacuation took place in the spring, Mother's Day flower crops, the best of the year, were abandoned or sold at rock-bottom prices. A strawberry grower pleaded with the government to let him harvest his crop. When he was denied permission, he

Japanese-American families such as this one were forced to sell off many of their belongings and move to relocation centers.

plowed it under. The FBI charged him with an act of sabotage and sent him to jail.[4]

Some of the losses were heartbreaking. Evacuees could not bring their pets with them. Yoshiko Uchida gave her dog, Laddie, to a college fraternity. "Be a good boy now, Laddie. We'll come back for you someday," she told the collie. Laddie died a week later.[5]

Some lucky Issei and Nisei knew trustworthy whites. These friends took care of their property during the war. Others were not so fortunate. Many had no such friends and lost virtually everything. Others put their trust in people who cheated them out of their property.

Once they sold their property, the Issei and Nisei packed up what was left. The necessities—sheets, blankets, pillows—went inside the evacuees' suitcases or bags. Letters, stuffed animals, photographs, toys—the personal items that make a house a home—stayed behind.

Then they rode or walked to the assembly points. Most dressed up for the occasion, as though they were going to church. Yoshiko Uchida's mother wore a hat, gloves, good coat, and Sunday gloves. Yoshiko wrote, "she would not have thought of venturing outside our house dressed in any other way."[6]

Not every white person or institution was heartless. Universities often gave Nisei students credit for the remainder of their terms. Most promised that these students could return at the end of the war. Friends cooked farewell meals for their departing neighbors and drove them to the gathering spots.

Those were unusual experiences. Ben Takeshita recalled that none of his former friends and neighbors would speak to him as he left. "They were afraid of being accused of being Jap lovers."[7]

"We took whatever we could carry," one evacuee lamented. "So much we left behind, but the most valuable thing I lost was my freedom."[8]

International Reaction

Civilians of Japanese ancestry were not displaced just in the United States. If anything, governments of other Western Hemisphere nations treated the Japanese worse than the United States did.

Mexico created a 100-kilometer (62-mile) evacuation zone along its Pacific Coast. Japanese, both citizens and

A World War I veteran wears his uniform as a protest while leaving for an assembly center.

aliens, were removed from the Baja California peninsula and moved inland. Mexican army troops guarded the coast in case of enemy attack.

Canada forced more than twenty-two thousand people of Japanese ancestry from their homes in British Columbia. Many were moved to camps, where they helped to build a highway through the Rocky Mountains. Men were separated from their families in these camps. After they left the coast, the government, which had promised to guard their land, sold it. The displaced Japanese were not allowed to vote or to serve in the Canadian Army.

Riots by Japanese residents rocked Peru after it was rumored that a Japanese Peruvian would be deported to Japan. An American representative who went to the South American country to see if there were signs of pro-Japan activity by the local Japanese population found none.

Nevertheless, the American and Peruvian governments agreed to the deportation of Japanese Peruvians to camps in the United States. The families of the imprisoned men were "invited" (forced) to join them. After it was determined that they were not dangerous enemy aliens, they were deported back to Peru—on the grounds that by leaving Peru (even though unwillingly), they had violated immigration laws.[9] In many cases, they found that Peru no longer wanted them. They were returned to the United States and in many cases obtained United States citizenship.

Ironically, the territory with the largest Japanese population saw the least discrimination. More than one third of all residents of Hawaii had some Japanese ancestry. Japanese labor was considered vital to the civilian and military economies of the Hawaiian Islands. Besides, the views of Delos Emmons, military commander of Hawaii, were the opposite of those of General DeWitt.

The federal government did not intend to operate mass concentration camps, Emmons told Hawaiians. "No person, be he citizen or alien, need worry, provided he is not connected with subversive elements."[10]

Other government officials tried to pressure Emmons into removing all Japanese Hawaiians to the mainland. He refused. "The feeling that invasion is imminent is not the belief of most of the responsible people," he commented. "There have been no acts of sabotage committed in Hawaii."[11]

Nevertheless, more than one thousand Hawaiians of Japanese descent were shipped to mainland camps. None were tried for espionage, much less convicted. In fact, only ten people were convicted by the United States government of spying for the Japanese during World War II. All ten were white.

Assembly Centers

At San Francisco, California; Los Angeles, California; and Seattle, Washington, assembly posts, a sea of people and luggage awaited transportation to points unknown.

A bewildered-looking girl, sitting among her family's belongings, awaits assignment to an assembly center.

Evacuation authorities offered storage for evacuees' possessions. Many had no alternative. They placed their spare possessions in government warehouses or garages, at the sole expense of the owner. If they were fortunate, the possessions were still there intact when they returned years later. Not everyone was fortunate.

Buses hauled the evacuees to the assembly centers that would be their temporary homes. Most passengers were silent, sad, bewildered, disappointed, bitter, and angry.

Most of the assembly centers were fairgrounds, livestock pavilions, or racetracks remodeled to hold the Japanese-American detainees. In 1941, many had gone to these places as customers. Now they were entering as prisoners.

"Multimillion-dollar Santa Anita racetrack—the world's most beautiful and luxurious racing plant—yesterday opened its gates as an assembly center for Japanese evacuees," *The Los Angeles Times* announced on April 4, 1942. "As nearly as possible, the evacuees will live lives as normal as can be arranged under the circumstances."[12]

The reporter might not have thought it "normal" if he or she had to live in the center. Santa Anita's "apartments" were former horse stalls, housing tenants named Whirlaway, War Admiral, or Gallant Fox. Most apartments had less than two hundred square feet of space. Straw-filled mattresses were used as beds. Meals were all served in communal mess halls. Poor sanitary conditions caused outbreaks of diarrhea.

Everybody had to wait. One resident recalled, "We lined up, for mail, for checks, for meals, for showers, for washrooms, for laundry tubs, for toilets . . ."[13]

Privacy ceased to exist. Laughter, crying, arguments, snores, sneezes, and conversations of a private nature traveled through the plywood walls. Minoru Yasui recalled, "It was like a family of three thousand people camped out in a barn."[14] Miyo Uchiyama recalled, "You could see between the slats of the buildings. . . . I really felt sorry for some of the teenagers, especially the shy ones. . . . I recall one of the girls lost her mind."[15]

Worst of all was the prison atmosphere. High barbed wire fences surrounded the centers. Each corner had a guard tower. The War Relocation Authority claimed that the evacuees were kept in assembly centers "for their own protection." An evacuee questioned, "If it was for our protection, why did the guns point inward, rather than outward?"[16]

Instant Communities

Despite the hardships, rules, and discomfort, the evacuees did what seemed impossible: They created communities.

Fortunately, most families and neighborhoods were moved together to nearby centers. Once evacuees got settled in their new surroundings, they looked for their friends. Then they tried their best to re-create the lives that were taken from them.

Christian churches and Buddhist temples were set up almost immediately. Schools started, although they lacked books, paper, chalk, and space. Newspapers were begun at some of the centers. Santa Anita published the *Pacemaker*, a free weekly paper. Chris Ishii, a former artist with Walt Disney studios, created L'il Neebo, a Nisei cartoon character, for the *Pacemaker*.

Sports took the time of many evacuees. What had been a weekend hobby could now become a full-time obsession. Before they entered the Merced evacuation center, Masao Hosina reminded his team, the

Livingston Dodgers, to bring their baseball uniforms and equipment with them. The team, which compiled a 34–4 record over the previous three seasons, continued its winning ways at Merced.

If anything, the camp was a boon for the players, said Gilbert Tanji. "We'd win so many games [at Livingston] that pretty soon nobody came to watch us play. So when we go into camp there was more competition—it was more fun."[17]

Baseball was the most popular sport, but evacuees participated in many others, including basketball, volleyball, and sumo wrestling. Actors and musicians entertained their fellow inmates with musicals and talent shows. Artists and craftspeople displayed their work.

Farmers and gardeners soon produced a variety of flowers and vegetables. The infield at Santa Anita was turned into a huge garden. A group of men at Tanforan made a small park with trees, a waterfall, and a small lake.

There were even special occasions. After one wedding at Tanforan, the bride and groom borrowed a staff member's car. They drove a few laps around the racetrack, then settled into married life in a horse stall. Several college students received their diplomas by mail at the centers. One student won a medal for high scholastic achievement. A local newspaper noted that the student could not attend the award ceremony because "his country had called him elsewhere."[18]

Some of the camps' activities were ironic. At

Camp inmates engaged in many activities. These four musicians form a makeshift band.

Tanforan, residents celebrated Flag Day in 1942. They sang "America the Beautiful" and recited the Pledge of Allegiance, honoring a country that was treating them anything but honorably. At the Santa Anita and Manzanar centers, Nisei made camouflage nets. These nets, deemed essential to the war effort, were constructed by citizens who were considered too dangerous to be left free on the outside.

Most found that their friends on the outside had not forgotten them. "There were all sorts of white

Women at the Manzanar camp assemble a camouflage net.

people who brought food and presents," said Shig Wakamatsu.[19] At first, the visitors were allowed to see their interned friends only from outside the barbed wire fences. Later, the centers created special visiting rooms.

The evacuation centers were intended for short-term stays, yet some were inhabited for more than eight months. Just as residents were becoming used to this life, they were moved once again. Their new homes would be even more forlorn and desolate.

THEY WERE CONCENTRATION CAMPS

Once again, the Issei and Nisei traveled. Now they were going to camps called relocation centers.

These evacuation centers were never meant to be long-term facilities. They were temporary detention sites that housed internees until more permanent camps could be built. Most evacuation centers were located near cities that formerly had significant Japanese-American populations. The relocation centers were built near mountains, sand, and sagebrush.

By isolating Issei and Nisei from other people, the government intended to minimize the chance of espionage by Japanese saboteurs. The isolation could also help avoid negative publicity that might come from the government holding innocent people as prisoners.

Yoshiko Uchida rode with her family in a rickety train to Utah. During the day, they passed by sites they had not seen for months—houses, trees, stores, white children. By night, they saw nothing. Guards ordered everyone to close their shades between dusk and dawn. They took no chances on Japanese saboteurs flashing secret messages in the dark.

At the Salt Lake City station, an old friend greeted Yoshiko. It was a fellow Nisei who voluntarily had evacuated to Utah several months earlier. The meeting made no sense. Her friend was free to do anything except return to the West Coast. Uchida could not even leave her train car.[1]

Uchida's train went to Delta, Utah. There the evacuees boarded buses that traveled into the middle of a desert. There, in land "dry as a bleached bone,"[2] lay the camp known as Topaz. Camp directors called it "the jewel of the desert."[3]

Topaz was one of ten out-of-the-way relocation camps. The others were Manzanar and Tule Lake, in California; Minidoka, Idaho; Heart Mountain, Wyoming; Granada, Colorado; Poston and Gila River, Arizona; and Rohwer and Jerome, Arkansas. Manzanar had been in use as an evacuation center; all the others were newly built. In addition to these camps, there were also special internment camps where troublesome evacuees were held.

"All ten sites can only be called godforsaken," wrote historian Roger Davis. "They were in places where nobody had lived before and no one has lived since."[4] Tule Lake, Minidoka, and Heart Mountain had severe winters. Temperatures would plunge to 30 degrees below zero at Heart Mountain. In the summertime, Poston and Gila Ridge evacuees roasted in temperatures above 100 degrees. Poston saw temperatures as high as 130 degrees. Rohwer and Jerome were located near Arkansas swamps, full of mosquitos and some of the most deadly rattlesnakes in North America. In Manzanar, near California's Death Valley, the swirling winds created blizzards in the winter and duststorms the rest of the year.

Even so, small cities grew up in these places. Topaz, with eight thousand residents, immediately became the fifth largest city in Utah. Manzanar, capable of holding ten thousand, was the largest city between Los Angeles and Reno, Nevada. Capacities ranged from eight thousand (Granada and Topaz) to twenty thousand (Poston), although camps often exceeded their intended capacities. Manzanar, at six thousand acres, was the smallest camp. Poston, at seventy-two thousand, was the largest.

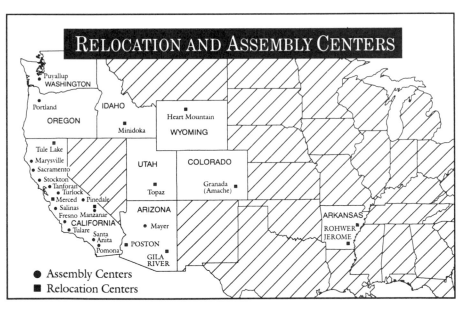

This map shows the locations of the ten permanent relocation centers set up for Japanese Americans. Many of these camps were located in areas with extreme weather conditions.

More than one hundred twenty thousand people lived in the camps. Two thirds of them were United States citizens. Almost all were of Japanese ancestry, but many non-Japanese spouses of evacuees chose to join their spouses and children in camps. Manzanar had an orphanage. Orphaned children from as far away as Alaska and with as little as one-sixteenth Japanese blood were placed there. No one explained how Alaskan orphans with one Japanese great-grandparent could pose a threat to national security.

Barracks

"When the bus stops, its forty occupants quietly peer out to see what Poston is like," a traveler recalled. "People look tired and wilted, with perspiration running off their noses. . . . Nevertheless, there are remnants of daintiness among the women and all are smiling . . ."[5]

Newcomers to Poston and the other camps lined up at long tables. War Relocation Authority employees filled out forms and took fingerprints, gave housing assignments, and administered physical examinations. The WRA officials asked the newcomers about their previous jobs and skills. Anyone who had a skill needed in camp was assigned to work immediately.

The living quarters were an improvement over the horse stalls of Santa Anita or the pigpens of Puyallup, Washington. Yet they were anything but luxurious. Most camps followed roughly the same pattern.

Topaz, for example, had forty-two blocks, each with twelve barracks. Each barrack was built with quarter-inch boards over a wooden frame. The outsides of the barracks were covered with tar paper nailed to the roof and walls. In the center of each block were a mess hall, washroom, and laundry barrack.

Each barrack had six rooms. The rooms were roughly twenty by twenty-five feet. They were furnished with nothing except four cots. Like the assembly centers, the camp apartments had no kitchens, bathrooms, or bedrooms, and little or no privacy. According to army regulations, camp housing was suitable only for combat-trained soldiers, yet half of the camps' population were women and one fourth were school-aged children. Some families lived in these conditions for more than three years.

White employees of the camps were not subjected to the same restrictions as their "guests." White apartments had running water, kitchens, all the lumber they needed, and even air conditioning.

Families immediately tried to make their dwellings livable. Men and women gathered scrap lumber abandoned by construction workers. From it, they made chairs, shelves, or tables. Many built closets and partitions to make bedrooms. Some even built porches outside their barracks. While this work took place, other family members began cleaning out the ever-present dust.

Once families set up their new homes, they were free to do virtually everything they wanted, except leave camp. Even the appearance of an escape attempt could be fatal. An old man at Topaz who wandered too close to the perimeter fence did not hear a guard's warning and was shot to death. He was picking up seashells and arrowheads.

Concentration Camps

These camps were not as severe as the death camps run by the Nazis. In Germany, innocent civilians performed slave labor. Sadistic doctors performed ghastly medical "experiments" with unwilling subjects. Millions of people were put to death in these Nazi concentration camps.

But there was one important similarity. Jews and gypsies were sent to the Nazi death camps because of their ancestry. In America, people were placed in the camps because they had Japanese ancestry. The WRA called them relocation centers. However, another term was more commonly used. "I'm for catching every Japanese in America, Alaska, and Hawaii, and putting them in concentration camps," said Congressman John Rankin. "We picked [the Japanese] up and put them in concentration camps," wrote United States Supreme Court Justice Tom Clark. "They were concentration camps. . . . We were in a period of emergency, but it was still the wrong thing to do," said Harry Truman, who became president when Roosevelt died. "Men and women who knew nothing of the facts . . . hotly deny that there are concentration camps. Apparently that is a term to be used only if the guards speak German and carry a whip as well as a rifle," wrote socialist reformer Norman Thomas.[6]

These people did not live in the camps. Kenneth Matsushige, a Heart Mountain veteran, did. "They had the army all the way around you, just like, well they were *concentration camps* more or less," he said. "They didn't call it that really, but relocation made it sound better."[7]

Keeping Busy

"[W]e had absolutely nothing to do," recalled William Hohri. "So what sets in is bordom. We used to play these long games of chess, four hours, one game of chess. Then we'd say, 'Let's play again.' There was nothing to do."[8]

Eventually, most evacuees shook that boredom. Many continued the activities of their previous free lives and the assembly centers. The actors returned to acting, the gardeners planted new seeds, and the Lexington Dodgers continued to win baseball games. The camps' greater space led to new activities. Some roamed the desert grounds looking for arrowheads or fossils or interesting stones. "We would play near barbed wire. We weren't supposed to, but we did," said Hiroshi Kanno, who lived in the Minidoka camp. "There was a target range not far from us. I can remember hunting around us for bullet shells."[9]

Camps set up schools, and children up to age sixteen were expected to attend. Vocational and adult education programs served older camp members.

Some centers had small gardens planted by the evacuees.

Both Nisei and white teachers taught basic reading and math skills. They also instructed students on how to act and what to say when they returned to the outside world. All classes were taught in English.

The camps had limited self-government. Block representatives formed community councils. Only Nisei could serve on the councils, but anyone sixteen or older could vote. For some Issei, it was the first time they could vote in an American election.

Judicial committees settled disputes within a camp. Three Nisei and three whites chosen by the camp director served on each committee. They recommended actions to the project director, who usually followed the recommendations.

Block managers took care of day-to-day functions in the camp. They supervised general maintenance of grounds and buildings and informed residents of new rules and regulations made by the camp administration. Older, respected Issei usually held these positions.

Dillon Myer claimed that the councils served as a communications link between residents and administration, that they also enforced ordinances in the interest of the community. Myer's critics pointed out that councils had only advisory, not decision-making, powers. Community government, they said, was a way to get inmates to do most of the camp's housekeeping chores for a low wage.

Workers

All communities need workers to keep themselves operating. Like outside communities, the relocation camps needed doctors, cooks, farmers, teachers, and people who held dozens of other jobs. The Issei and Nisei became those workers.

Residents received wages for performing their tasks, but the pay was poor and workers seldom were paid on time. Myer feared an outcry if workers received as much as a soldier's twenty-one-dollar a month pay. So unskilled workers earned twelve dollars a month, professionals got nineteen dollars, and everyone else received sixteen. Later, the twelve-dollar pay scale was omitted and the nineteen-dollar rate was expanded to include also "those making exceptional contributions."

The rates were grossly unfair. Nisei doctors in camp hospitals who earned nineteen dollars a month worked alongside white doctors who earned their normal pay—more than fifty times as much as the Nisei.

Myer hoped to establish active agricultural and industrial communities in the camps, but the idea never came to pass. Local businesses feared competition from the camps' cheaper-wage workers. Workers in the camps made some products, but most of the goods were made only for camp consumption. There were sawmills at Heart Mountain and Jerome, a mattress factory in Manzanar, garment factories in Manzanar, Heart Mountain, and Minidoka, and other various shops everywhere.

Workers pooled their money and formed cooperatives that helped residents form small businesses, from shoe repair shops to dry goods stores. Most of the cooperatives were well-managed and very successful. They provided employment for more than seven thousand residents, did more than $22 million worth of business, and paid out $2.3 million in refunds to cooperative members.

Outside groups noted the evacuees' success. Sears Roebuck and Company advertised its mail order business in some camps' newspapers. Other companies followed its example. The Bank of America opened a branch in the Manzanar camp.

Threats to Families

Some positive results came from the relocation camps. For the first time, Nisei could assume leadership roles.

The Bank of America opened a branch at the Manzanar camp.

They did not have to defer to the older Issei. Nisei students were no longer outnumbered minorities. They could star on baseball teams or edit the school yearbook. Those with professional skills were not kept out of the workforce. Teachers could teach and doctors could practice. Older residents, used to a lifetime of twelve-hour workdays, could take some well-earned rest.

But the camps extracted their toll in other ways. Japanese family life had kept communities together. Camp life threatened the family system. Husbands no longer were the breadwinners because the camp provided basic services such as food and medicine. There was no real opportunity for economic gain. As a result, many evacuees lost incentives for advancement.

Families no longer ate at home, but in mess halls. Children ate with their friends, not their parents. Younger ones did not remember private meals. When they played house, they lined up for meals instead of pretending to cook.

Teenagers who had spent after-school hours helping their parents now had time on their hands. Before the war, juvenile delinquency was virtually unknown among Japanese-American youngsters. In the camps, they started forming gangs.

Resentments between generations emerged. On the outside, the older Issei had made all the decisions. Because they were United States citizens, the Nisei assumed authority in the camps. Some Nisei were disrespectful to the Issei. The Issei ridiculed the Nisei because their citizenship did not keep them from being held in the camps.

In some camps, evacuees spent evenings sitting around campfires. Issei might sit around one fire, remembering the way things were and blaming Nisei for their current miseries. Another campfire might find young Nisei radicals ready to go on strike or beat up suspected informers. Other Nisei would gather at another fire, irritated both at the Issei who disdained them and the Americans who imprisoned them.

These groups had resentments that smoldered under the surface. In some camps, the resentments would flame into violence.

6

WHAT'S THIS CAMP COMING TO?

Under a calm surface, tensions boiled in the camps. There was resentment against the low pay, the unappetizing food, the crowded bathrooms. Most of all, evacuees resented the lack of freedom. They hated the censorship that authorities forced upon them. White camp employees read evacuees' incoming and outgoing mail. Camp residents published newspapers, but they were subject to review by the camp directors. The *Manzanar Free Press* was free in name only.

Under these conditions, people became suspicious of each other. Anyone could be an informer, a spy for the administration. Resentments flared against the informers, the camp administration, the United States government that kept them prisoner, and the American people who allowed the government to oust them from their homes. These demonstrations took the form of protests and strikes.

Poston

Hooded assailants cornered Kay Nishimura at Poston on November 14, 1942. They beat the suspected informer almost to death. Authorities suspected that the camp's judo club was a headquarters for administration haters. Fifty judo club members were rounded up, but they soon were released. The following night, the parents of another suspected informer were beaten. Judo club members George Fujii and Isamu Uchida were rearrested.

WRA director Dillon Myer visited the camp the next day. Camp director Wayne Head, Myer, and other top officials left the camp a few hours later. Soon, a crowd gathered in front of the camp jail. They shouted speeches in favor of the imprisoned "judo boys." They denounced informers, whom they called *inu* (dogs).

John Evans, the next in command, let the Issei protesters speak; then he addressed the assembled evacuees. Evans asked everyone to remain calm, but his translator did not repeat the director's remarks. Instead of relaying what Evans had said, he called for release of the prisoners and a strike by camp residents.

At nightfall, soldiers marched to Poston's gates. Some militants wanted to fight the troops. Fortunately, cooler heads prevailed. Troops and guns withdrew. Both prisoners eventually were released. Dislike, distrust, and irritation remained, but the bullets stayed outside of the camp.

Manzanar Massacre

Hatred burned almost immediately at the Manzanar camp. Pro-American, pro-administration members of the JACL formed one faction. A group of *Kibei* (American-born people educated in Japan) were on the other side.

Manzanar residents had reason for discontent: White camp employees were stealing their food. Sugar and other supplies were rationed throughout the United States, and many Americans were willing to pay high prices for the scarce black market goods. The employees cheated camp residents out of part of their food supplies, took the surplus into nearby towns, and sold the stolen food at black market prices.

Evacuee Henry Ueno monitored the sugar thefts. When he found the camp's sugar supply to be 6,100 pounds short in October 1942, Ueno confronted camp officials. They promised to make up the shortage in November; Ueno, however, noted continuing food thefts. Instead of being grateful for Ueno's alertness, camp officials considered him a troublemaker.

The food crisis erupted on December 4, 1942. "Food was being taken out of camp not by one carton but by the truckloads," noted Tom Watanabe. "The white drivers coming in were stealing the food. . . . [Ueno] was keeping a record of it and they snatched him."[1]

Ueno spent the night in jail in nearby Independence, California. Meanwhile, six masked men beat up a JACL leader believed to be an informer. Several suspects were arrested.

Government agents then returned Ueno to Manzanar and threw him into the camp jail. These arrests drew protests. Hundreds of evacuees gathered outside the administration building. Military police quickly surrounded them. With rifles and tear gas, the troops were prepared for attack. Then someone threw a lightbulb at the military patrol. It shattered, causing a shot-like sound.

The MPs responded by hurling tear gas canisters at the evacuees. "That smoke just covered the whole area," Ueno recalled. "A sergeant taking charge in front was yelling, 'Remember Pearl Harbor, hold your line.' . . . And [at] the same time, before the gas is cleared, they start shooting."[2]

Two lay dead and ten injured after what became known as the Manzanar Massacre ended. Authorities tried to cover up the incident. A board of inquiry from army headquarters in San Francisco tried to persuade witnesses to say that the dead and injured evacuees were threatening or attacking the military police. However, the investigation of the trajectory of the bullets showed that they had been shot in the side or the back. When the hospital's chief surgeon was asked to alter the medical records, he refused and was fired the next day.

Pro-American ringleaders were shipped off to one work camp; their foes were shipped to another. Ueno was kept in isolation at the second camp. When FBI agents came to question him, he repeated the accusations of theft by Manzanar employees. "That's a very serious charge," he was told. "If your statement's wrong you could be in serious trouble."

Ueno answered, "I know, but I'm right." The FBI

investigated and never bothered him again. Ueno figured that they must have discovered the wrongdoing.[3]

No-Nos

On January 28, 1943, Secretary of War Stimson declared, "It is the inherent right of every faithful citizen, regardless of ancestry, to bear arms in our nation's battle."[4] President Roosevelt added, "No loyal citizen of the United States should be denied the democratic right to exercise the responsibilities of his citizenship, regardless of his ancestry."[5]

For some Nisei, the announcements were a blessing. They loved the United States and wanted to fight for their country. Others were less enthusiastic. They had volunteered for the armed forces after Pearl Harbor. Instead of being in combat, they found themselves behind barbed wire.

The WRA felt Nisei in combat would be good for public relations. Some government officials had their doubts. The War Department decided to have every adult Japanese take a loyalty test to separate patriots from potential troublemakers. A loyalty registration form was created to determine which Japanese Americans wanted to serve in the armed forces, and which wanted to be released for war-related work. WRA director Dillon Myer called the loyalty question "a bad mistake" but went along with the idea.

Issei and adult Nisei soon received loyalty questionnaires. Question 27 asked Nisei men if they would volunteer for combat in the armed forces (Nisei women and Issei were asked to volunteer for nursing or auxiliary units). Question 28 asked if they would swear allegiance to the United States.

WRA officials assumed people would give unquestioning positive responses to questions 27 and 28. They were wrong. Issei balked at answering question 28. They were not eligible for United States citizenship. If they renounced the only country that allowed them to be citizens, they would be stateless people.

Many Nisei, on the other hand, fumed when they were asked to renounce allegiance to Japan. They were Americans, not Japanese citizens. Togo Tanaka refused to renounce allegiance to the Japanese emperor. Tanaka explained, "we never owed him allegiance. So how could we renounce it?"[6] Question 28 was later changed to "Will you swear to abide by the laws of the United States and take no action which would in any way interfere with the war effort of the United States?"

SOURCE DOCUMENT

26. Have you ever applied for repatriation to Japan?

27. Are you willing to serve in the armed forces of the United States on combat duty, wherever ordered?

28. Will you swear unqualified allegiance to the United States of America and faithfully defend the United States from any or all attack by foreign or domestic forces, and forswear any form of allegiance or obedience to the Japanese emperor, or any other foreign government, power, or organization?

Questions 27 and 28 had to be answered in the presence of army recruiters. The registration form was mandatory except for people seeking repatriation to Japan. Even so, the response disappointed the WRA. Many irate evacuees refused to answer the questionnaire altogether. Some answered No to questions 27 and 28; they became known as No-Nos.

Others found different ways to protest. One man, a Yes-Yes, asked the army representative if he was a citizen. Yes, came the reply. Then he asked, "May I go to Phoenix?" No, he could not, because the Arizona city was part of the restricted area. Then he tore up the questionnaire. "That's the way I feel about your attitude toward our citizenship," he responded.[7]

It was hoped that thirty-five hundred Nisei registrants would volunteer for the army. Instead, only twelve hundred volunteered. WRA officials did not expect opposition to the loyalty oath. In some camps, opposition to the oath became a matter of honor.

Rejecting the Military

Reactions to the registration varied from camp to camp. Topaz evacuees sent a petition to the War Department asking for full restoration of civil rights before they would register. The government responded that registration was a "crucial test" for the evacuees and it was no time "to quibble or bargain." The committee that drew up the petition urged Topaz residents to register. They did, but 32 percent of the men answered No to question 28.

In Minidoka, Nisei men who answered Yes to questions 27 and 28 were immediately whisked over to "voluntary induction." Only 7 percent of male Nisei in Minidoka answered No to the controversial questions. About three hundred young men from Minidoka volunteered. The camp, which had only 7 percent of the total evacuee population of the camps, had 25 percent of the volunteers.

Hecklers at Poston bombarded government officials with pointed questions: Why were loyal Japanese Americans not allowed back in California? Why couldn't Nisei soldiers visit the camp? Why were Nisei draftees kicked out of the military after December 7, 1941? Why were veterans of the last war, who already had proved their loyalty, put into camps?

Jerome evacuees were threatened with imprisonment if they failed to register. Eventually, everyone registered. Many answered No to question 28.

At Manzanar, Issei flocked to sign forms for repatriation to Japan. The rush became so intense that authorities stopped handing out repatriation requests until the registration period ended. Issei, meanwhile, urged their Nisei children to respond No to 27 and 28. After question 28 was revised so that Issei would not have to renounce foreign ties, most changed their answers to Yes.

Tule Lake presented problems to the WRA from the beginning. Tuleans heard of the upcoming registration at the end of January 1943. They heard that registration would not be necessary for people who applied for repatriation to Japan.

Community council members tried to get information from the camp director about the registrations. Instead, the director stalled until the actual registration began.

The evacuees remained uncertain of why they had to register and how the registration would proceed. They were angry about the injustice of imprisoned citizens having to join the military and the possibility of forced resettlement. When the JACL met in early February and favored voluntary enlistment and reinstatement of the draft for Nisei, rumors arose that the JACL and Tule Lake administrators were responsible for the registration. Army team members and WRA officials met with evacuee groups on February 9. They read a prepared War Department statement. Few officials accepted questions from the evacuees. Those that did gave only prepared responses that did not answer the questions.

Few Tuleans registered. Some who did tried to withdraw those registrations. Instead, they wrote petitions complaining about the registration. Officials still refused to answer direct questions about the registrations. Instead, they threatened antiregistration leaders with fines and prison sentences. Later, when those same officials learned from the FBI that there was no law against refusing to participate in the loyalty oaths, they never bothered to relay that information to the evacuees.

At first, registration was done at the individual housing blocks. Administrators feared that block pressure might keep some evacuees from registering, so they changed the registration site to the administration area. The change made no difference. On February 18, the army and internal security officers appeared at the mess hall and read off the names of those who had not registered. They warned of sedition (treason) penalties for those who would not cooperate. The next day, trucks arrived to take registrants to the administration office. No one boarded them. Two days later, military police charged into block 42, picked up the uncooperative Nisei, and trucked them off to nearby county jails.

The arrests frightened some residents. For others, the arrests only strengthened their resistance. Many requested repatriation to Japan. The army countered that it was a "mistaken idea" to assume that such a request exempted anyone from having to register. This ruling contradicted earlier statements that those seeking repatriation would not have to register.

Antiregistrants now had another issue: They would not cooperate until the arrested resisters were returned to camp. Authorities refused to return the arrested men, to promise that there would be no further arrests, and to stop having teachers put pressure on their students to change No answers to Yes.

By now, the camp was hopelessly divided into two factions. Those who registered were considered to be inu (dogs). They were isolated at mess hall tables.

Children made barking sounds when they saw them. Some were beaten by Kibei.

The lack of cooperation embarrassed army officials at Tule Lake because the army was not meeting its quota of registrants here. They offered a compromise: Anyone who registered and answered No to 27 or 28 would not have to enter the military. This offer also failed. When the registration period ended, only one third of Tulean men and half of the women had registered. More than three thousand people refused to sign the loyalty oath.

Camps would be in turmoil if "loyal" Yes-Yes and "disloyal" No-No Japanese and Japanese Americans were kept together. Senator Albert "Happy" Chandler suggested to Myer in April that "disloyal" enemies be separated from residents of other WRA centers. Project directors, meeting in May, unanimously backed Chandler's suggestion.

They chose Tule Lake as the site of the segregation camp. The California camp was large enough to accommodate all of the so-called disloyals from the other camps. Besides, far more opposition came from Tule Lake than from any other camp. If Tule Lake was made the segregation camp, these rebels need not be moved.

In the summer of 1943, the transfers took place. Many but not all "loyal" Tule Lake residents went to other camps. They were replaced by "disloyal" residents of other camps and their families. Fifteen thousand people were moved in and out of Tule Lake.

Nisei board a boat for Japan. Hundreds of Japanese Americans who renounced their United States citizenship while in the evacuation camps were sent back to Japan.

There were other additions to Tule Lake as well: a new eight-foot fence around the camp, six new tanks, and new barracks built to house one thousand additional military troops.

An unhealthy mix of people now inhabited the camp. Some were people who wished to return to Japan. Others wrote No or refused to register because they did not wish to serve in the military. Some remained embittered at being detained by the United States government. Some wrote No because they did not wish to be separated from their families. In some cases, aging Issei parents who counted on their children for support did not want to risk losing sons in combat. They urged their children to write No.

Basically "loyal" people also inhabited Tule Lake.

Some were family members who came along with their No-No relatives. Some were neutral but wrote No under pressure from family or friends. There were also Tule Lake residents who wrote Yes to questions 27 and 28 but did not feel like moving from the camp.

Martial Law at Tule Lake

Conditions were already ripe for trouble at Tule Lake. Thoughtless administrators and bad luck only made them worse.

In October 1943, the administration fired forty-three workers who protested the discharge of three colleagues for insubordination. These firings led to a strike. The administration rehired the fired workers, and the strike stopped. Soon afterward, a farm truck returning to camp turned over. One man was killed and five were injured. Camp workers blamed the careless driver. The accident led to a work stoppage of eight hundred people.

Tuleans wanted a large public funeral for the dead worker, but project director Ray Best refused. Despite his refusal, the funeral went on as planned. When mourners snatched a camera from an administration officer ordered to photograph funeral organizers, Best shut off electricity to the assembly hall where the funeral was taking place.

Meanwhile, Best made arrangements to harvest the crops. He announced that striking farmworkers were fired and arranged for loyal farmers to be brought in from other camps. These unknowing strikebreakers were paid the prevailing local wage, one dollar an hour. Tule Lake farmworkers had been paid only sixteen dollars a month.

Furthermore, the strikebreakers received food taken illegally from the Tule Lake warehouses. This theft enraged Tule Lake residents, who already faced food shortages.

WRA director Dillon Myer was scheduled to visit Tule Lake on November 1, 1943. After he entered the administration building, five to ten thousand demonstrators surrounded it. He agreed to meet with the camp's negotiating committee.

Meanwhile, a different group went to the camp's medical office and attacked a doctor. This renegade group had nothing to do with the negotiating committee, but when Best heard of the attack, he suspended negotiations. He refused to discuss termination of workers, their replacement by workers from other camps, and the use of food from Tule Lake warehouses to feed the strikebreakers. Myer addressed the crowd, then left. Two days later, an order was issued that prohibited large public gatherings.

Japan and the United States had no diplomatic relations because they were at war. The Spanish consul handled Japan's diplomatic affairs. The consul met with Tule Lake officials to resolve camp problems. The November 4 meeting was interrupted when someone reported that white camp employees were moving more food out of the camp. That news started fights between them and the evacuees. Best called in the army.

The army took over and declared martial law. An already repressive atmosphere became worse. A Nisei girl wrote, "After the Army came in, I really felt like a prisoner. . . . There were no activities. Everything stopped. We had a curfew . . . we got baloney for Thanksgiving."[8]

Word of the martial law reached Japan. Japanese radio reported, "The American Army has entered the Tule Lake Center with machine guns and tanks and is intimidating the residents."[9]

The army sought out and arrested antiadministration leaders. Rebels in the camp passed around a petition supporting the negotiating committee. A young Nisei who signed against her will remembered, "If you didn't sign it the next thing you know, you'd be beaten to a pulp."[10]

In early December, Tuleans voted on a general strike by all camp members. The general strike was defeated, but those already striking stayed away from their jobs. After the Spanish consul had no luck with the administration, he suggested to the negotiating committee that they give up. Instead of getting the original detainees released, more rebels were being rounded up every day.

On January 11, 1944, Tule Lake residents voted on whether to continue the partial strike. Busy soldiers rounded up dozens of people known to favor the strike who might have made the difference in the election. By a margin of 473, Tule Lake residents voted to end the strike. After that vote, the army ended martial law and returned the camp to civilian control.

Some Nisei found military combat to be an impossible idea, given their prisoner status at home. Others, who considered military service their patriotic duty, joined all-Nisei units which became legendary in American warfare.

THE 442ND REGIMENT

Despite protests that took place at many camps, most Nisei filled out the registration forms and declared Yes-Yes to questions 27 and 28. Army recruiters instantly signed up many of these Nisei. They had several reasons for volunteering. Many felt driven by a sense of patriotism. Others felt that military service was a way of proving their loyalty to America. Some thought that volunteering for the armed forces might improve their families' chances of leaving the camps. Some just wanted to get out of the camps themselves.

On January 28, 1943, the 442nd Combat Team started operations. It was a six thousand-man, all Nisei unit. Dillon Myer at first did not want a segregated unit, but later admitted that the 442nd had proved to be a good idea. "America's conscience would not have been so dramatically reawakened on the Japanese American question as it was during the latter part of the war if Nisei had merely been scattered through the armed forces," he said.[1]

The 442nd trained in Camp Shelby, Mississippi. Soon the 100th Battalion, an all-Nisei National Guard unit from Hawaii, joined them. Then they moved across the Atlantic Ocean.

Both units saw action in Europe in the fall of 1943. The 100th left first and took part in the invasion of Italy. The 100th soon became known as the Purple Heart Battalion because of the many casualties it suffered. Casualties mounted so high that it had to be reinforced by the 442nd.

"Go for broke" was the motto of the 442nd, squad member Daniel Inouye said. Inouye, who later became a United States senator from Hawaii, explained that it meant to give "everything we had; . . . to scramble over an obstacle course as though our lives depended on it; . . . to march quick-time until we were ready to drop . . ."[2]

DeWitt's Downfall

The thought of Japanese in the military nearly made General John DeWitt explode. Nisei in service would refute his belief that no person of Japanese ancestry could be loyal to the United States.

Public opinion turned against DeWitt when he opposed Nisei soldiers visiting the West Coast on leave. DeWitt declared, "I don't want any of them here. They are a dangerous element."[3]

The Washington Post countered, "The general

should be told that American democracy and the Constitution of the United States are too vital to be ignored and flouted by a military zealot."[4] After a while, the War Department agreed. By autumn of 1943, the department relieved DeWitt of the Western Defense Command.

Nisei and the Draft

Nisei troops in the 442nd and 100th were so effective that in early 1944, the War Department declared that all male Nisei could be drafted. However, despite the records achieved by the Japanese-American soldiers, the government still would not treat Nisei as the equals of other Americans. Prospective Nisei inductees received different questionnaires than did non-Japanese. They were asked about loyalty to Japan and were made to renounce allegiance to Japan.

Many refused to fill out the insulting documents, and some were arrested for draft evasion. Judge Louis Goodman sympathized: "It is shocking to the [American] conscience that an American citizen be confined on the ground of disloyalty, and then, while so under duress and restraint, be compelled to serve in the armed forces or be prosecuted," he commented.[5]

Not all judges held the same view as Goodman. In May 1944, sixty-three Heart Mountain draft resisters were arrested. All were convicted.

European Heroism

Meanwhile, the Nisei troops in Europe continued to serve with honor. After only a few months in Italy,

Japanese-American troops march through a European town. The all-Nisei 442nd was the most decorated outfit in American military history.

the 442nd had earned more than a thousand Purple Hearts and seventy-four other decorations. By mid-1944, the 100th had become part of the 442nd.

The unit moved up Italy and then traveled to the Vosges Mountains of France. There they had their finest hour. In October 1944, they liberated the Lost Battalion, a Texas unit trapped behind German lines. It took 800 Nisei dead and wounded (a 60 percent casualty rate) to rescue the 211 men.

From there, the 442nd returned to Italy, where

they performed another incredible feat. Allied forces had tried to break through the Gothic Line for six months with three divisions—forty thousand men. The 442nd accomplished the feat in less than an hour.

The 442nd also helped liberate prisoners from the concentration camp at Dachau, Germany. They freed others even while their own families were trapped behind barbed wire. A fifteen-year-old blindfolded Polish girl awaited execution when German troops suddenly abandoned the camp. Finally, someone took off her blindfold. What she saw shocked her. "'It's the Japanese come to kill us,' she thought. 'Just kill us,' she said. 'Get it over with.'" The Nisei soldier assured her, "You are free."[6]

The Asian War

Seven thousand miles from Europe, Nisei troops served as translators, interpreters, and spies for American combat units. Their skills were invaluable. Colonel Sidney F. Mashbir, commander of the Asiatic Theater Intelligence Service, commented, "thousands of American lives were preserved and millions of dollars in material were saved as a result of [Nisei] contribution to the war effort."[7]

The Army Intelligence Service needed men who could speak Japanese to serve as scouts and interpreters. Thousands of Nisei volunteered for the assignments. Most volunteers were so Americanized that only one tenth of the first thirty-seven hundred interviewed knew enough Japanese to qualify for the training.

Those who passed the tests went to a language school in Minnesota; then they went to assignments in the Pacific. More than sixteen thousand Nisei served in the Pacific. They were so valuable that white troops were assigned to guard them from Japanese attack.

The Nisei questioned prisoners, translated documents, and intercepted radio messages. They captured documents that revealed the Japanese battle plans for the Philippines. When American troops invaded, they knew the enemy plans by heart.

Some Nisei in the Pacific won notable honors. Ben

SOURCE DOCUMENT

Every Marauder knows [the Nisei] . . . This is due to the courage and bravery shown by them. One of our platoons owe their lives to Sergeant Hank G. who translated [Japanese] orders. . . . we called him 'Horizontal Hank' because he has been pinned down so many times by Jap machine gun fire. The boys who fought alongside of Hank agree that they have never seen a more calm, cool, and collected man under fire . . . the Marauders want you to know they are backing the Nisei 100 percent.[8]

Nisei soldiers in the Pacific also saw combat. One white soldier with Merrill's Marauders fought with Nisei in Burma and India. He commented on his comrades.

Kuroki flew fifty-eight combat missions and won three decorations. Kenny Yasui, pretending to be a Japanese colonel, captured sixteen enemy soldiers by ordering them to drop their weapons and surrender to American troops.

Many Gold Stars

Nisei glory came at a high price. More than thirty-three thousand Nisei served in the United States Army. No other similar ethnic group had a greater commitment. More than ninety-four hundred Nisei were dead or wounded by war's end. "[We] had a heavy burden to prove ourselves," said Shigeo Wakamatsu. "World War II changed things for the better—at a great cost of men's lives."[9]

Gold stars, symbolizing a fallen loved one, decorated barracks at Granada or Minidoka as well as other American homes. One Issei Gold Star mother lamented, "I cannot describe in words the sadness I feel at the time I received the notice of Kiyoshi's death in Italy. It is difficult for me to comprehend that my son volunteered and died fighting for the very country whose leaders treated his parents so badly because we were Japanese."[10]

Ten Thousand Purple Hearts

The 442nd became known as the Christmas tree regiment because of the many honors it received. Nisei in the Pacific also won well-deserved honors for their heroism. Altogether, Nisei won thousands of awards. These included seven Distinguished Unit

Citations, one Congressional Medal of Honor, a Distinguished Service Medal, 52 Distinguished Service Crosses, 22 Legions of Merit, 28 Oak Leaf Clusters to the Silver Star, 1,200 Oak Leaf Clusters to the Bronze Star, 360 Silver Stars, 4,000 Bronze Stars, and nearly 10,000 Purple Hearts.[11]

President Harry S Truman welcomed the 442nd to the White House on July 15, 1946. He told them, "You fought not only the enemy, but you fought prejudice and you have won."[12]

8

While Nisei were fighting on European or Pacific battlefields, another type of battle was taking place in American courtrooms. Four very different Nisei young adults sought to end many of the injustices against Japanese Americans. Their cases met with varying results.

THEIR JOB WAS TO UPHOLD THE CONSTITUTION

Minoru Yasui

Minoru "Min" Yasui was a patriot. He served in the Army Reserve Corps while he was in college. After receiving his law degree, the Oregon native went to Chicago and worked with the Japanese consul. He resigned the day after the Pearl Harbor attack. Yasui could have stayed in Chicago. If he had done so, he would have escaped the punitive laws against Japanese Americans. But his father told him that military service was his patriotic duty. A few days later, the FBI took the older man to an internment camp.

Min Yasui returned to his hometown, Hood River, Oregon. He was drafted in December 1941. When he reported and an army recruiter saw that he was Japanese, he was not accepted.

Then he went to Portland. In March 1942, General John DeWitt issued Military Proclamation Number 3: All German enemy aliens, all Italian enemy aliens, and all persons of Japanese ancestry had to obey an 8:00 P.M. to 6:00 A.M. curfew. They had to remain within five miles of their home or business unless they had special military permission.

"It seems to me that no military commander should have the authority or power to designate certain rules and regulations for the civilian population to follow in the absence of martial law," Yasui explained years later. "A military order distinguishing between one citizen on one hand and another on the basis of ancestry was absolutely wrong."[1]

Yasui decided to challenge the curfew. On the night of March 28, he walked into a nearby police station and surrendered. Two days later, he left on bail. Yasui ignored notices ordering anyone of Japanese descent in Portland to report to an evacuation center. Instead, he returned to Hood River. Military police arrested him there a few days later and took him to Portland's assembly center. He and other Portland area evacuees were sent to the camp at Minidoka, Idaho.

When the date for Yasui's trial came, military police escorted him to Portland. He rode unrestrained in the car. At nightfall, they did not stop in a restaurant. Instead, the military police officer dropped Yasui off in the nearest jail. The next day, in Portland, Judge James Alger Fee sentenced Yasui to a year in jail and a five thousand dollar fine.

Yasui spent most of the next year in a six-by-eight-foot Portland jail cell. Meanwhile, his lawyers appealed the case all the way to the Supreme Court where he lost his case. Justices there ruled that DeWitt's orders were valid and enforceable.

By August 1943, Yasui had served out his jail sentence. The judge waived the fine. Of course, he still was not free. Upon leaving jail, he was driven back to the Minidoka camp.

He did not stay there long. Camp officials released him so that he could recruit Nisei for the army. Yasui traveled around Colorado, Wyoming, and Nebraska, urging Nisei to show their loyalty by registering for the draft. His message, "Have faith in America," convinced very few people. Knowing the injustices heaped upon Nisei and Issei on the West Coast, Nisei did not rush to help the government that had imprisoned them.

Gordon Hirabayashi

Gordon Hirabayashi was a student at the University of Washington. Like Yasui, he chafed at the idea of a curfew for those of Japanese ancestry. Why should he be confined while his classmates, including some Canadians, walk freely? He challenged the curfew. "The first [curfew] violation came when I decided to behave like an American, like the rest of my dorm mates."[2]

Hirabayashi worried about his parents' fate. "Legally and technically they were enemy aliens," he said.[3] They and other Issei urged him to worry about himself. "Some of the more cynical Issei said, 'If anything happens to us, you'll be there with us,'" Hirabayashi recalled.[4] They were right.

Like Yasui, he refused to follow expulsion orders when they came. He noted, "If I refused to comply with curfew, how could I go through with this order. . . . I prepared a statement to hand to the FBI when the time came."[5]

He originally planned to take the case to the American Civil Liberties Union (ACLU), but the national ACLU refused to take his case. "Apparently there were too many loyal supporters of Franklin D. Roosevelt who did not want to obstruct his war program," Hirabayashi guessed later.[6]

Hirabayashi surrendered in May 1942. He spent five months in jail awaiting trial; then a lower court found him guilty. In July 1943, the Supreme Court heard the case. The highest court, too, found him guilty. He was sentenced to three more months in jail.

"I expected us to lose at the lower court level. But when the case reached the Supreme Court, I somehow felt that those nine men up there were different, that they were objective," Hirabayashi recalled. "Their job was to uphold the constitution. I couldn't see how they could approve this order."[7]

Fred Korematsu

Fred Korematsu had no plans to be part of a court case. The Oakland, California, welder wanted to remain outside the evacuation centers, with his white girlfriend. He was fired from two welding jobs because of his Japanese ancestry. So he used a false name and changed his facial features through minor plastic surgery in order to avoid detection.

Korematsu evaded capture for two months. On May 30, 1942, he was arrested. His girlfriend, persuaded by her family and intimidated by the FBI, broke up with him.

Once inside the evacuation center, Korematsu decided to fight his captivity. "There was a lot of pressure on Fred from other internees. They said, 'Don't rock the boat,'" said attorney Peter Irons.[8] That pressure only made Korematsu more determined.

He went to the northern California chapter of the American Civil Liberties Union. As with Hirabayashi, the national ACLU warned the northern California chapter not to take the case, but they took it anyway. Korematsu was found guilty on September 8 of remaining in an evacuation area contrary to an exclusion order.

The case reached the Supreme Court in December 1944. Hundreds of thousands of Japanese Americans, both in and out of relocation camps, anxiously awaited the Court's ruling.

They were disappointed. The Supreme Court ruled 6–3 that the exclusion of civilians from a military zone was legal. The majority of judges believed the military authorities' words that it was impossible to segregate loyal Issei and Nisei from disloyal ones. Justice William O. Douglas wrote, "Korematsu was not excluded from the Military Area because of hostility to him or to his race."[9]

Justices Owen J. Roberts, Robert Jackson, and Frank Murphy wrote bitter dissents. Roberts commented, "It is a case of convicting a citizen . . . for not submitting to imprisonment in a concentration camp solely because of his ancestry."[10] Jackson added that if DeWitt's evacuation order was constitutional, "then we may as well say that any military order [in wartime] will be constitutional and have done with it."[11] Murphy called DeWitt's order "legalization of racism."[12]

Mitsuye Endo

The same day that Fred Korematsu lost his Supreme Court case, Mitsuye Endo won hers. The victory led to the release of thousands of people.

Mitsuye Endo was a twenty-two-year-old California resident who lost her state job as a stenographer in early 1942 because of her Japanese ancestry. Endo went when she was ordered to the Tanforan assembly center. She did not resist when she was moved to the Tule Lake camp. But she contacted the Japanese American Citizens League. The JACL contacted lawyers who agreed to take the case.

Mitsuye Endo seemed like the perfect candidate for a test case. She had a good background. Her brother was in the Army, and her parents had never returned to Japan. She represented loyal Japanese Americans. Unlike Fred Korematsu, who tried to evade the law, Mitsuye Endo obeyed it. The attorneys petitioned for a writ of habeas corpus, a court decision that would declare that she could not be imprisoned without being tried and convicted of a crime.

She had refused opportunities to leave Tule Lake. Voluntary departure from the camp might hurt her case. Finally, the case was called to the Supreme Court. She was surprised that the case went to the nation's highest court.

Endo had a number of allies. One of them was WRA director Dillon Myer. He hoped Endo would win the case. A definite Supreme Court ruling might end the internments altogether.

Justice Department attorneys, representing the government, realized that they had a hopeless case. The government had to defend Executive Order 9066, which had allowed the military to remove Issei and Nisei from the West Coast. The order was based almost entirely on General DeWitt's final report; yet they knew that Navy and FBI intelligence reports contradicted DeWitt, whose statements were considered to be purposely incorrect. Yet the government persisted. Yielding on the Endo case without a struggle would have meant confessing to a mistake that had disrupted a hundred thousand lives and cost millions of dollars.

The Supreme Court unanimously ruled in favor of Endo: Loyal citizens could not be imprisoned indefinitely. The Court ruled that the internment process was constitutional, however. That ruling made little difference. The day before the decision was made, the Western Defense Command revoked the mass exclusion order.

Now Issei and Nisei could return home to the Pacific Coast, and many did. Before the Endo ruling, most of the people who left the relocation camps moved to the Midwest or East. After Endo's ruling, most Japanese Americans went to California, Oregon, Washington, and Arizona.

In a way, WPA director Dillon Myer got his wish. The days of the camps would soon be over.

A BLOT ON THE HISTORY OF OUR COUNTRY

Although he was the director of the War Relocation Authority, Dillon Myer did not believe that the law-abiding Issei and Nisei should be held against their will. But the camps were there, and someone had to direct the WRA. If he did not do it, someone less sympathetic to the internees would take his place.

Myer cited several reasons for helping inmates leave: He realized that Japanese Americans would not remain loyal Americans if they were kept captive. Deviation from normal lives would have a bad effect, especially on children. Myer did not want to establish a new set of reservations in the United States.

The WRA called the camps relocation centers, and Myer wanted them to live up to the name. Under his plan, evacuees would stay in camps until they could find work outside the evacuation zones. The WRA would help them move into their new surroundings.

Four groups of Japanese Americans gained quick release. The first were Japanese linguists needed in the war effort. About five thousand translators and

A young resident of the Rohwer camp examines the graves of some of his relatives.

interpreters went overseas, despite General DeWitt's objections.

The second group were college students, who would be the Japanese-American leaders after the war. The young Nisei could not return to their universities on the Pacific Coast, but they could study at any eastern or midwestern college that would accept them.

Since the government offered no scholarships to these Nisei, students had to pay their own tuition. This was difficult for families whose property had been confiscated by the government. The students also had to find a school. Many schools, such as Princeton and the Massachusetts Institute of Technology, refused to take them. Some turned down the Nisei, claiming they had "military installations on campus."[1] Eventually, 143 institutions of higher learning accepted 3,500 evacuee students.

Agricultural workers also got temporary releases from camps. They were needed because of the labor shortage caused by the war. In May 1942, the first group was released from a Portland assembly center to harvest sugar beets. By the end of the year, ten thousand others would be released from camps to do farmwork.

Their situation was unusual. Many of the farmworkers had owned farms before the evacuation order. Had they been left alone, they would be the landowners paying others to harvest their crops.

There was one other irony. Evacuee farmers were required to be in the camp area at night, unless accompanied by their employers or a government official, but other Japanese Americans living in the area had no restrictions at all.

Like the students, the agricultural workers were peaceful. There is no record of attempted escape by any of the farmworkers. Yet these releases bothered some diehard Japanese opponents. In 1942, the American Legion passed a resolution protesting the release of the college students and farmworkers.

The final group that received early clearance were

part of the Japanese-American civilian exchanges. More than two thousand civilians were sent to Japan. Most were diplomats or prisoners.

Leave Clearance

In the summer of 1942, permanent work leaves began. Camp inmates could work outside if state and local officials agreed that their labor was needed. The employers had to provide housing and transportation, and they had to pay the prevailing wage without displacing local workers. Local law authorities had to assure the workers' safety.

Inmates could leave if they had job offers or other means of support. The WRA also needed evidence that they would not endanger national security and that their presence would be accepted by the surrounding community. They were required to keep the WRA informed of any change of address.

Myer called the policy leave clearance. At first, it went anything but smoothly. It involved a lot of paperwork and security clearances from the FBI. Eventually, the process was speeded up. Evacuees could leave the camp almost immediately.

The WRA opened up offices in Chicago and Salt Lake City in early 1942 to help evacuees find work. By the end of the year, more than twenty other offices opened in eastern and midwestern cities. These offices worked with local businesses to hire the Nisei. Often they had great success. Chicago alone offered more than ten thousand jobs.

Most of the evacuees went to eight states—Illinois, Colorado, Ohio, Utah, Idaho, Michigan, Minnesota, and New York. In some cases, the relocation could be an advantage. One Nisei in Chicago wrote to the president of the University of California, "Hundreds of Japanese Americans are employed in occupations which were denied to them on the Pacific Coast. They have, for the first time, found occupation outlets . . ."[2]

West Coast officials remained opposed to having Japanese Americans in their states. Earl Warren, then governor of California, claimed "No one will be able to tell a saboteur from any other Jap."[3]

Racism was not confined to the West Coast. In Chicago, some cemeteries refused to bury Japanese corpses. Some dance halls would not admit Japanese customers. The same hospitals that welcomed Japanese Americans as employees turned them away as patients.

Despite the problems that might lie ahead, most Nisei jumped at the chance to leave the camps. "I felt wonderful the day I left camp," Helen Murao remembered. "We took a bus to the railroad siding and then stopped someplace to transfer, and I went in and bought a Coke, a nickel Coke. It wasn't the Coke, but what it represented—that I was free to buy it."[4]

Closing the Centers

By 1944, attitudes in Washington, D.C., were changing. With the overbearing DeWitt gone, top Washington officials now spoke their minds to President Roosevelt. Attorney General Francis Biddle told him, "the present practice of keeping loyal American citizens in concentration camps for longer than is necessary is dangerous and repugnant to the principles of our Government."[5]

On June 2, 1944, Secretary of the Interior Harold Ickes recommended that the relocation centers be closed. He listed his reasons to the president: The War Department assured Roosevelt that there was no danger to national security. Exclusion was clearly unconstitutional. Exclusion of Issei and Nisei from the West Coast made it more difficult to relocate them elsewhere. The longer the evacuees stayed in the camps, the more difficult it would be for them to readjust to normal life.

"I will not comment at this time on the justification or lack thereof for the original evacuation order," Ickes wrote. "But I do say that the continued retention of these innocent people in the relocation centers would be a blot upon the history of this country."[6]

Roosevelt hesitated. He did not campaign for the end of West Coast exclusion. A presidential election was coming up in November 1944. Return of the Nisei might displease California voters, and Roosevelt believed that he needed California's electoral votes to win the election.

Evacuation Revoked

By mid-1944, the tide of war had changed. Allied troops now had a strong foothold in Western Europe. American forces had the Japanese on the run in the

Pacific. The war was far from over, but it was only a matter of time.

In the United States, the relocation centers also had changed. Most young, loyal, and able adults were out of the camps now, working elsewhere. The camps remained as storehouses for children, the elderly, and at Tule Lake, for malcontents. One camp, Jerome, closed in late June.

On December 17, 1944, one month after Roosevelt's reelection and one day before the Endo Supreme Court decision, the War Department revoked its evacuation orders. Evacuees would be free

Evacuees wish their friends well as the Jerome camp closes.

to return to California, Oregon, Washington, and Arizona. The next day, the WRA announced that remaining relocation centers would be closed by the end of 1945.

Many evacuees were delighted with the news; others saw problems. Most evacuees had suffered mental anguish and financial losses. They feared physical violence if they returned home. Almost every Buddhist priest had been removed from the Pacific Coast, and many Buddhist evacuees wished to stay where they could worship. Some families had become accustomed to group living and did not want to change their lifestyle. Chizuko Omorl recalled, "A young woman was so afraid to leave the camp to face a hostile white society that she became unbalanced and bashed her baby's brains out with a hammer."[7]

Tule Lake's camp posed special problems. Residents of the other camps were considered loyal. They could leave the camps without posing security problems. But Tule Lake housed the No-Nos who had refused to sign loyalty oaths Many of them, under pressure from camp radicals, had signed forms renouncing United States citizenship. Some had second thoughts and now wished to reclaim their citizenship. Most evacuees, no matter what their status, worried about being separated from their families.

Every other camp was closed by the end of 1945, but Tule Lake had more than seven thousand people remaining. By March 1946, five thousand had been transferred to internment camps. The rest were mainly elderly, impoverished, or mentally ill people.

On March 20, 554 evacuees were still in Tule Lake. By the end of the day, they had left their "home" of more than three years. On March 21, 1946, the population of Tule Lake was zero.

WE SHOULD PARDON THE GOVERNMENT

A single atomic bomb was dropped on Hiroshima, Japan, on August 6, 1945. It exploded with a force greater than ever before known to humanity. Three days later, a larger blast leveled the port of Nagasaki. These atomic bombs marked the end of the Japanese empire. World War II was over.

By now, many Japanese Americans had returned to the West Coast. Some of them returned to nothing. Their trusted "friends" had sold their possessions. Goods believed safe in warehouses had been stolen or vandalized. Their land had fallen into other people's hands because trusted partners failed to pay real estate taxes.

Prejudice against Issei and Nisei had not disappeared with the war. Returning evacuees faced shootings, bombings, and arson. More than thirty such incidents were recorded in the late 1940s. The Arizona state legislature passed a bill that would have made it virtually impossible for any Issei or Nisei to buy goods in the state. A court ruling voided the law.

Gradually, anti-Japanese attitudes changed. Bigots

On August 9, 1945, the United States dropped a bomb on Nagasaki, Japan.

still existed on the West Coast, but they no longer made the rules. A turning point came in late 1945.

Mary Masuda's brother had died a hero's death on an Italian battlefield, earning a Distinguished Service Cross. When Mary returned home to California, however, she received neither sympathy nor welcome. Instead, neighbors threatened her.

General Joseph Stillwell tried to defuse this hatred. He flew across the country to present Mary Masada with her brother's medal. Americans throughout the country heard of the presentation from newspapers and newsreels.

Many evacuees returned home to find the goods that they had left behind were stolen or vandalized.

The publicity helped quell anti-Japanese feeling. When California voters had a chance to pass restrictive anti-Japanese laws in 1948, the measures failed overwhelmingly.

Other laws began to right wrongs against people of Japanese ancestry. President Harry S Truman urged Congress to pass the Japanese American Claims Act of 1948. It was hardly a generous appropriation. Congress gave only $38 million to cover twenty-three thousand claims totaling at least $131 million.

Four years later, Congress passed the Walter-McCarran Act. Thousands of Issei, aliens in their adopted land for most of their lives, now became United States citizens. That same year, the Alien Land Law was declared unconstitutional. Those Issei who were not yet citizens could legally own land for the first time in forty years.

Repatriation

Other injustices remained uncorrected for many more years. One such group of injustices had been inflicted on repatriates at Tule Lake.

Rumors flew at Tule Lake and the other camps that all Issei would be shipped to Japan. Their Nisei children, rather than separate from their parents, asked for repatriation.

Others signed up for repatriation involuntarily. A rebel group that called themselves *Sokuji Kihoku Honshi Dan* (Organization to Return Immediately to the Homeland) terrorized other camp residents. Dressed in headbands and gray sweatshirts printed with red rising suns, the symbol on the Japanese flag, they exercised at dawn while screaming pro-Japanese slogans. These hotheads encouraged other Tuleans to file for repatriation. Some were afraid to disobey them.

In the spring of 1944, the pro-Japanese group wanted to take over the camp. They demanded the ouster of pro-American evacuees. Camp administrators had a different idea. They would transfer the anti-American protesters to internment camps. Then those who requested repatriation could be shipped to Japan. Loyal evacuees would take over the camp, and eventually it could be closed.

There was one catch. The Nationality Act declared that a United States citizen could only renounce citizenship by applying to a consul while abroad; no one could renounce citizenship while in the United States. Congress in 1944 repealed that part of the act, then the Justice Department approved all renunciation requests.

In July 1945, President Truman signed Presidential Regulation 2655. It declared: "All dangerous enemies . . . who adhered to enemy governments . . . shall be subject to removal from the United States."[1]

Many of those who had given up their United States citizenship now had second thoughts. They wanted no part of a one-way trip to war-ravaged Japan. Thousands protested, saying their renunciations had been made under pressure.

Japanese-American war veterans march, seeking rights for themselves and their families.

Wayne Collins, a San Francisco attorney, had been the lawyer for Fred Korematsu in his unsuccessful evacuation challenge. He wrote a nineteen-page letter to Attorney General Tom Clark. The letter said that renunciation did not automatically make evacuees Japanese. Instead, they were stateless victims of coercion by the government and by organized gangs.

The attorney filed a lawsuit in November 1945, claiming that these people were still United States citizens. Their renunciations were not valid because they had no opportunity to consult lawyers or invite witnesses. Collins also claimed that the congressional amendment to the Nationality Act was unconstitutional.

More than thirty-five hundred plaintiffs sued to regain their United States citizenship. In 1949, Judge Louis Goodman ruled that each case must be tried separately. Collins protested in vain. For the next two decades, he worked to secure full citizenship rights for these Nisei clients.

The final court action took place on March 6, 1968. A weary Collins savored his victories. After the last verdict he commented, "This brings to a conclusion these . . . proceedings. . . . The episode which constituted an infamous chapter in our history has come to a close."[2]

Justice for Korematsu

Fred Korematsu strode into Oakland's courthouse on November 10, 1983. Nearly forty years earlier, courts had ruled against him when he tried to stay out of a relocation camp. After the 1944 Supreme Court case he had married, returned to California, and worked as a draftsman until his retirement.

Attorney Peter Irons called Korematsu in 1982. Irons had discovered new evidence in the case and offered to challenge the Supreme Court verdict.

Irons and Korematsu's other attorneys charged that the government had lied to the Supreme Court. Government lawyers had suppressed, altered, and destroyed key evidence.

Government attorneys approached Korematsu

with the idea of offering him a pardon. One Korematsu attorney recalled, "Fred Korematsu said, 'We shouldn't accept a pardon. If anything, we should pardon the government.'"[3]

Irons told the court that the government had withheld evidence that the Nisei were overwhelmingly loyal as a group. The government lawyers also presented false evidence of supposed acts of espionage by Japanese Americans. In 1982, Fred Korematsu said:

> As long as my record stands in federal court, any American citizen can be held in prison or concentration camps without a trial or hearing. . . . I would like to see the government admit they were wrong and do something about it, so this will never happen again to any American citizen of any race, creed, or color.[4]

His conviction was later overturned. Min Yasui and Gordon Hirabiyashi also were cleared in later hearings.

Redress

For nearly four decades, Issei and Nisei remained silent about their wartime experience. In the late 1970s, they began to make their discontent known. They sought redress (compensation) for injustices that were done. White America was now more willing to support them.

Thirty-four years after President Franklin D. Roosevelt signed Executive Order 9066, another president revoked the order. In 1976, Gerald Ford declared, "Not only was that evacuation wrong, but Japanese Americans were and are loyal Americans."[5]

Ford's successor, Jimmy Carter, also sympathized. He created the Presidential Commission on the Wartime Relocation and Internment of Civilians (CWRIC). In 1983, the commission published its final report, *Personal Justice Denied*. It called for a formal apology by Congress, a presidential pardon for persons who ran afoul of the law while resisting wartime restrictions, and a one-time, tax-free payment of twenty thousand dollars to each surviving Japanese American who had been interned. The first two issues met with no opposition. The third faced a struggle.

The Japanese American Citizens League sought a monetary compensation bill in 1970. The civil rights group asked for money, tax-free, based on the number of days each person was held. The bill went nowhere. In 1979, United States representative Mike Lowrey proposed a bill offering fifteen thousand dollars per evacuee plus fifteen dollars for each day served. This bill, too, failed to find support.

A redress bill passed the House of Representatives in 1987 and the Senate also passed it a few months later. President Ronald Reagan signed the Civil Rights Bill of 1988 on August 4, 1988. It contained a formal government apology but no funds for internees.

In late 1989, Senator Daniel Inouye added redress funds to another bill. This time, Congress passed the monetary compensation bill. President George Bush signed the appropriations bill on November 21, 1989.

Checks went to camp survivors, in order of age. Reverend Manoru Eto, a 107-year-old man, received the first check. At least half of the victims of Executive Order 9066 did not live to see the bill passed. They received neither an apology nor a penny from the government.

The Price They Paid

The evacuees went on with their lives after the camps closed. Some became quite successful. Shigeo Wakamatsu became a doctor, and served as president of the Japanese American Citizens League. Gordon Hirabayashi served as professor of sociology at the University of Alberta. Yoshiko Uchida wrote dozens of books, including some about her wartime

President Ronald Reagan signs the Civil Rights Bill of 1988, which apologizes to Americans of Japanese descent for their wartime detention.

internment experience. Yuki Okinaga, the bewildered-looking girl pictured at an evacuation point, became an assistant dean at the University of Illinois.

But even those who made material gains lost because of the war. They lost most or all of their property. Some estimated the Japanese American losses were six billion dollars.

They were not the only losers. The rest of America spent millions of dollars to build the camps, and to feed, house, and guard the evacuees. They also lost the brainpower and labor of hardworking, innocent civilians who were treated as traitors.

Those one hundred twenty thousand evacuated people lost something even more important than money—time. Paul Shinoda commented, "I lost about five years—I just lost them. . . . The sad part of it is, there's no glory in being evacuated, you can't say I'm an evacuee—veteran of the evacuation."[6]

Protect All Citizens

The redress movement and court decisions had an important result: the determination that injustices such as those imposed upon Japanese Americans would never be repeated.

Judge Marilyn Hall Patel summed up the danger when she commented on the Fred Korematsu case:

> Our institutions must be vigilant in protecting constitutional guarantees . . . our institutions, legislative, executive and judicial, must be prepared to exercise their authority to protect all citizens from the petty fears and prejudices that are so easily aroused.[7]

★ TIMELINE ★

1884—More than two hundred fifty immigrants, most students, move from Japan to the United States.

1905—Japan defeats Russia in Russo-Japanese War. Anti-immigrant and anti-Japanese groups start forming in California.

1906—San Francisco transfers Japanese students from its white schools to segregated schools in Chinatown.

1913—California enacts the Alien Land Law, prohibiting aliens ineligible for citizenship from owning land.

1941—*December 7*: A Japanese air armada destroys much of the Pearl Harbor Naval base, causing the United States to enter into World War II.

1942—*February*: Japanese fishermen and their families are forcibly removed from Terminal Island.

1942—*February 19*: President Franklin D. Roosevelt signs Executive Order 9066, giving the military the right to exclude "any or all persons from designated areas, including the California coast."

1942—*March 2*: General John DeWitt declares two military zones, covering most of the West Coast.

1942—*March 18*: Executive Order 9012 establishes the War Relocation Authority, the governing body for Issei and Nisei evacuees.

1942—*March 27*: DeWitt issues Public Proclamation Number 4, prohibiting Issei and Nisei from leaving Military Zone 1.

1942—*March 28*: Minoru Yasui is arrested for violating curfew in Portland, Oregon. He fights and loses the case in the Supreme Court.

1942—*April 30*: Fred Korematsu is arrested for violating evacuation orders.

1942—*June 2*: DeWitt declares the entire West Coast an evacuation area.

1942—*June 3*: Japan suffers a crushing defeat at the Battle of Midway. This loss ends any chance of a Japanese invasion of America.

1942—*Spring*: The evacuation to assembly centers begins.

1942—*Fall*: Ten relocation camps open.

1942—*November 14*: Hooded assailants beat a suspected informer at the Poston camp. Soldiers suppress a potential riot.

1942—*December 4*: Military police kill two and injure ten during the "Manzanar Massacre."

1943—*January 28*: Secretary of War Stimson announces plans for a Japanese-American army unit, the 442nd regimental combat team. Soon afterwards, the army begins administering loyalty oaths to adult Japanese Americans.

1943—*Summer*: Issei and Nisei who are considered disloyal to America are transferred to Tule Lake.

1943—*October*: The firing of forty-three workers leads to a strike at Tule Lake. The strike lasts until January 1944.

1944—*December*: The War Department revokes its relocation order, thus allowing evacuees to return to the West Coast.

1944—*December 18*: The Supreme Court upholds the exclusion of Fred Korematsu from the Pacific Coast. The same day, the Court declares that Mitsuye Endo and other loyal citizens cannot be imprisoned indefinitely.

1945—*August 6*: The first atomic bomb is dropped on Hiroshima. Japan surrenders a few days later.

1945—*November*: Attorney Wayne Collins files the first lawsuit claiming that Issei and Nisei renunciations of United States citizenship are invalid. Thirty-five hundred such lawsuits take place over the next twenty-three years.

1946—*March 21*: Tule Lake, the last of the relocation camps, closes.

1952—*June 27*: The Walter-McCarran Act allows thousands of Issei to become United States citizens. The Alien Land Law is declared unconstitutional.

1976—*February 19*: President Gerald Ford revokes Executive Order 9066.

1983—*November 30*: Court overturns Korematsu conviction. Later hearings also clear Minoru Yasui and Gordon Hirabayashi.

1988—*August 4*: The Civil Rights Bill of 1988 contains a formal apology to Japanese and Japanese Americans interned during the war.

1989—*November 21*: President George Bush signs an appropriations bill granting $20,000 to each camp survivor.

★ CHAPTER NOTES ★

Chapter 1

1. Interview with Shigeo Wakamatsu, November 26, 1994.

2. Ibid.

3. Bill Hosokawa, *Nisei: The Quiet Americans* (New York: William Morrow and Company, 1969), p. 231.

4. Bernard Schwartz, *Super Chief: Earl Warren and His Supreme Court—A Judicial Biography* (New York: New York University Press, 1983), p. 17.

Chapter 2

1. John Armor and Peter Wright, *Manzanar* (New York: Times Books, 1988), p. 26.

2. Roger Daniels, *Prisoners without Trial: Japanese Americans in World War II* (New York: Hill and Wang, 1993), p. 10.

3. *Strength and Diversity: Japanese American Women 1885–1990*, exhibit, Field Museum of Natural History (Chicago: January–March, 1995).

4. Daniel S. Davis, *Behind Barbed Wire: The Imprisonment of Japanese Americans During World War II* (New York: E. P. Dutton, 1982), p. 18.

5. Yoshiko Uchida, *The Invisible Thread* (New York: Julian Messner, 1991), pp. 14, 55.

6. Daniels, p. 23.

Chapter 3

1. Roger W. Axford, *Too Long Been Silent: Japanese-Americans Speak Out* (Lincoln, Nebr: Media Publishing and Marketing Company, 1986), p. 40.

2. "Chronology of World War II Incarceration," *Japanese American National Museum Quarterly*, October–December, 1994, p. 12.

3. Paul Bailey, *City in the Sun: The Japanese Concentration Camp at Poston, Arizona* (Los Angeles: Westernlore Press, 1971), p. 3.

4. Ibid., pp. 32–33.

5. *Strength and Diversity: Japanese American Women 1885–1990*, exhibit, Field Museum of Natural History (Chicago: January–March, 1995).

6. Ibid.

7. Bernard Schwartz, *Super Chief: Earl Warren and His Supreme Court—A Judicial Biography* (New York: New York University Press, 1983), p. 15.

8. Yoshiko Uchida, *The Invisible Thread* (New York: John Messner, 1991), p. 67.

9. Robert Wilson and Bill Hosokawa, *East to America: A History of Japanese in the United States* (New York: William Morrow and Company, 1989), p. 192.

10. Roger Daniels, *Prisoners without Trial: Japanese Americans in World War II* (New York: Hill and Wang, 1993), pp. 25–26.

11. Ibid., p. 25.

12. Ibid., p. 30.

13. Daniel S. Davis, *Behind Barbed Wire: The Imprisonment of Japanese Americans During World War II* (New York: E. P. Dutton, 1982), p. 28.

14. G. Edward White, *Earl Warren: A Public Life* (New York: Oxford University Press, 1983), p. 73.

15. Ibid.

16. Schwartz, p. 16.

17. John Armor and Peter Wright, *Manzanar* (New York: Times Books, 1988), p. 20.

18. Daniels, p. 34.

19. Davis, p. 30.

20. Daniels, p. 40.

21. Ibid.

22. Davis, p. 37.

23. Ibid.

24. Daniels, p. 57.

25. "Chronology of World War II Incarceration," p. 12.

26. Daniels, p. 57.

27. Wilson and Hosokawa, p. 98.

28. *Unfinished Business: The Japanese-American Internment Cases*, Mouchette Films, 1984.

29. Interview with Shigeo Wakamatsu, November 26, 1994.

Chapter 4

1. Gordon Hirabayashi, "Why Review the Japanese American Wartime Crisis?" *Friends*, August 1–15, 1995, p. 4.

2. Daniel S. Davis, *Behind Barbed Wire: The Imprisonment of Japanese Americans During World War II* (New York: E. P. Dutton, 1982), p. 28.

3. Yoshiko Uchida, *Desert Exile: The Uprooting of a Japanese American Family* (Seattle: University of Washington Press, 1982), p. 24.

4. John Armor and Peter Wright, *Manzanar* (New York: Times Books, 1988), p. 5.

5. Yoshiko Uchida, *The Invisible Thread* (New York: Julian Messner, 1991), pp. 70–71.

6. Uchida, *Desert Exile*, p. 69.

7. John Tateishi, *And Justice for All: An Oral History of the Japanese American Detention Camps* (New York: Random House, 1984), p. 244.

8. Armor and Wright, front jacket.

9. Davis, pp. 54–55.

10. Armor and Wright, p. 164.

11. Ibid., p. 165.

12. Paul Bailey, *City in the Sun: The Japanese Concentration Camp at Poston, Arizona* (Los Angeles: Westernlore Press, 1971), p. 3.

13. Armor and Wright, p. 7.

14. Tateishi, p. 74.

15. Budd Fukei, *The Japanese American Story* (Minneapolis: Dillon Press, 1976), p. 55.

16. Armor and Wright, p. xii.

17. "Sport and Community in California's Japanese-American Yamoto Colony," *Journal of Sports History*, vol. 19, no. 2, Summer 1992, p. 139.

18. Uchida, *Invisible Thread*, p. 85.

19. Interview with Shigeo Wakamatsu, November 26, 1994.

Chapter 5

1. Yoshiko Uchida, *The Invisible Thread* (New York: Julian Messner, 1991), p. 93.

2. Yoshiko Uchida, *Desert Exile: The Uprooting of a Japanese American Family* (Seattle: University of Washington Press, 1982), p. 92.

3. Uchida, *The Invisible Thread*, p. 105.

4. Roger Daniels, *Concentration Camps USA: Japanese Americans and World War II* (New York: Holt, Rinehart and Winston, Inc., 1971), p. 96.

5. Dorothy Thomas and Richard Nishimoto, *The Spoilage: Japanese-American Evacuation and Resettlement During World War II* (Berkeley: University of California Press, 1969), p. 32.

6. James Hirabayashi, "'Concentration Camp' or 'Relocation Center', What's in a Name?" *Japanese-American National Museum Quarterly*, October–December, 1994, p. 9.

7. Roger W. Axford, *Too Long Been Silent: Japanese-Americans Speak Out* (Lincoln, Nebr.: Media Publishing and Marketing Company, 1986), p. 40.

8. Ibid., p. 22.

9. William F. Keefe, "The Ivory Curtain," *Oak Park Journal*, April 12, 1995, p. 12.

Chapter 6

1. John Tateishi, *And Justice for All: An Oral History of the Japanese-American Detention Camps* (New York: Random House, 1984), p. 97.

2. Ibid., p. 199.

3. Ibid., p. 203.

4. Dorothy Thomas and Richard Nishimoto, *The Spoilage: Japanese-American Evacuation and Resettlement During World War II* (Berkeley: University of California Press, 1969), p. 56.

5. Ibid.

6. Daniel S. Davis, *Behind Barbed Wire: The Imprisonment of Japanese Americans During World War II* (New York: E. P. Dutton, 1982), p. 88.

7. Ibid.

8. Ibid., p. 96.

9. Thomas and Nishimoto, p. 152.

10. Ibid., p. 157.

Chapter 7

1. Dillon Myer, *Uprooted Americans: The Japanese Americans and the War Relocation Authority During World War II* (Tucson: University of Arizona Press, 1971), p. 146.

2. Daniel S. Davis, *Behind Barbed Wire: The Imprisonment of Japanese Americans During World War II* (New York: E. P. Dutton, 1982), pp. 103–104.

3. John Armor and Peter Wright, *Manzanar* (New York: Times Books, 1988), p. 58.

4. Ibid., p. 59.

5. Davis, p. 106.

6. Gerald Parshall, "Freeing the Survivors," *U.S. News and World Report,* April 3, 1995, pp. 58–59.

7. Myer, p. 152.

8. Ibid., p. 151.

9. Interview with Shigeo Wakamatsu, November 26, 1984.

10. *Strength and Diversity: Japanese American Women 1885–1990*, exhibit, Field Museum of Natural History (Chicago: January–March, 1995).

11. Myer, p. 148.

12. Ibid., p. 149.

Chapter 8

1. *Unfinished Business: The Japanese-American Internment Cases*, Mouchette Films, 1984.

2. Roger W. Axford, *Too Been Long Silent: Japanese-Americans Speak Out* (Lincoln, Nebr.: Media Publishing and Marketing Company, 1986), p. 4.

3. *Unfinished Business.*

4. Ibid.

5. Axford, p. 5.

6. Ibid., p. 6.

7. Ibid., p. 7.

8. *Unfinished Business.*

9. Roger Daniels, *Prisoners without Trial: Japanese Americans in World War II* (New York: Hill and Wang, 1993), p. 61.

10. Ibid., p. 62

11. Ibid.

12. Ibid.

Chapter 9

1. John Armor and Peter Wright, *Manzanar* (New York: Times Books, 1988), p. 139.

2. Roger Daniels, *Prisoners Without Trial: Japanese Americans in World War II* (New York: Hill and Wang, 1993), p. 79.

3. Edward White, *Earl Warren: A Public Life* (New York: Oxford University Press, 1982), p. 73.

4. John Tateishi, *And Justice for All: An Oral History of the Japanese American Detention Camps* (New York: Random House, 1984), p. 48.

5. Armor and Wright, p. 60.

6. Dillon Myer, *Uprooted Americans: The Japanese Americans and the War Relocation Authority During World War II* (Tucson: University of Arizona Press, 1971), pp. 178–179.

7. Roger W. Axford, *Too Long Been Silent: Japanese-Americans Speak Out* (Lincoln, Nebr.: Media Publishing and Marketing Company, 1986), p. 108.

Chapter 10

1. John Christgan, *Enemies: World War II Alien Internment* (Ames, Iowa: Iowa State University Press, 1985), p. 166.

2. Ibid. p. 181.

3. *Unfinished Business: The Japanese American Internment Cases*, Mouchette Films, 1984.

4. Steven A. Chin, *When Justice Failed: The Fred Korematsu Story* (Austin, Tex: Raintree Steck-Vaughn Publishers, 1993), p. 92.

5. Yoshiko Uchida, *The Invisible Thread* (New York: Julian Messner, 1991), p. 132.

6. John Tateishi, *And Justice for All: An Oral History of the Japanese-American Detention Camps* (New York: Random House, 1984), p. 58.

7. Roger Daniels, *Prisoners without Trial: Japanese Americans in World War II* (New York: Hill and Wang, 1993), p. 100.

★ FURTHER READING ★

Armor, John, and Peter Wright. *Manzanar*. New York: Times Books, 1988.

Axford, Roger W. *Too Long Been Silent: Japanese-Americans Speak Out*. Lincoln, Nebr.: Media Publishing and Marketing Company, 1986.

Bailey, Paul. *City in the Sun: The Japanese Concentration Camp at Poston, Arizona*. Los Angeles: Westernlore Press, 1971.

Chin, Steven A. *When Justice Failed: The Fred Korematsu Story*. Austin, Tex.: Raintree Steck-Vaughn Publishers, 1993.

Christgan, John. *Enemies: World War II Alien Internment*. Ames, Iowa: Iowa State University Press, 1985.

Daniels, Roger. *Concentration Camps: North American Japanese in the United States and Canada During World War II*. Malabar, Fla.: Robert Krieger Publishing Company, 1981.

———. *Prisoners without Trial: Japanese Americans in World War II*. New York: Hill and Wang, 1993.

Davis, Daniel S. *Behind Barbed Wire: The Imprisonment of Japanese Americans During World War II*. New York: E. P. Dutton, 1982.

Delios, Hugh. "A 1940s Warning for 1990s." *Chicago Tribune* (March 12, 1995).

Fukei, Budd. *The Japanese American Story*. Minneapolis: Dillon Press, Inc., 1976.

Girdner, Audrey, and Ann Loftis. *The Great Betrayal: The Evacuation of the Japanese-Americans During World War II*. London: Macmillan, 1969.

Hirabayashi, Gordon. "Why Revive the Japanese American Wartime Crisis?" *Friends* (August 1–15, 1995).

Hosokawa, Bill. *Nisei: The Outlet Americans*. New York: William Morrow and Company, 1969.

Japanese American National Museum Quarterly (October–December), 1994.

Keefe, William F. "The Ivory Curtain." *Oak Park Journal* (April 12, 1995).

Masaoka, Mike, with Bill Hosokawa. *They Call Me Moses Masaoka*. New York: William Morrow and Company, 1987.

Myer, Dillon. *Uprooted Americans: The Japanese Americans and the War Relocation Authority During World War II*. Tucson: University of Arizona Press, 1971.

O'Brien, David J., and Stephen S. Fujita. *The Japanese American Experience*. Bloomington, Ind.: Indiana University Press, 1991.

Okimoto, David I. *Americans in Disguise*. New York: Walker/Weatherhall, 1971.

Parshall, Gerald. "Freeing the Survivors." *U.S. News and World Report* (April 3, 1995).

Schwartz, Bernard. *Super Chief: Earl Warren and His Supreme Court—A Judicial Biography*. New York: New York University Press, 1983.

Shimpo, Rufu. "Like Oil and Water." *Los Angeles Japanese Daily News* (June 1, 1995).

"Sport and Community in California's Japanese-American Yamoto Colony." *Journal of Sports History* (Summer 1992).

Tateishi, John. *And Justice for All: An Oral History of The Japanese-American Detention Camps*. New York: Random House, 1984.

Thomas, Dorothy, and Richard Nishimoto. *The Spoilage: Japanese American Evacuation and Resettlement During World War II*. Berkeley: University of California Press, 1969.

Uchida, Yoshiko. *Desert Exile: The Uprooting of a Japanese American Family*. Seattle: University of Washington Press, 1982.

———. *The Invisible Thread*. New York: Julian Messner, 1991.

White, G. Edward. *Earl Warren: A Public Life*. New York: Oxford University Press, 1983.

Wilson, Robert A., and Bill Hosokawa. *East to America A History of Japanese in the United States*. New York: William Morrow and Company, 1980.

★ INDEX ★